The "How To" book of making big money with rental homes

THIRD EDITION, REVISED

●

by Dave Glubetich
REALTOR

First printing 1975
Second printing 1976
Third printing 1977
Fourth printing 1978

© copyright 1978 Dave Glubetich
Library of Congress Catalog Card Number 75-20848
ISBN 0-9601530-1-2

The Monopoly Game
is available directly from
Impact Publishing Company
12 Gregory Lane
Pleasant Hill, California 94523
(415) 689-5090
$9.95

Printed in The United States of America

To Kathy,
Shelly,
and Steven

Acknowledgments

I wish to thank the following people for
their encouragement and technical help:
Lon Carlston, Merle Hall, Janet Hockaday,
Howard Pierce, David and Janet Williams,
Dave Wigginton, and Mildred Goodman of
Professional Publishing Corporation.

Contents

Introduction

I learned by losing. If I knew in 1965, when I began my real estate career, what I know today, I could be retired with a substantial monthly income.

. During my first year as a real estate salesman, I came across many fine investment buys, but I didn't really consider making a purchase. One I remember was a fine three-bedroom, two-bath, contemporary home. The owner wanted $1,000 to assume his 5¼ per cent GI loan of $21,000. Today this home could sell for about $43,000. I didn't act — I lost out. And I lost out on many others too, until I made my first investment purchase in 1968.

After getting my feet wet it became easy. Today I own 12 rental properties plus a gorgeous mountain home near Alpine County's Bear Valley ski resort. I have also bought and sold many other homes.

Not only do I now have thousands of dollars in equity, but my rental properties have helped me to reach a tax shelter level of over $30,000. Of course, three children and medical deductions help some. But the 12 properties account for more than $18,000 in deductions and my own residence brings in another $4,000. During 1977 my paper profits (increased value from appreciation plus increases in equity through shrinking loan balances) exceeded my income from my real estate business.

So let me show you how you can do it too. I'll help save you hundreds of dollars and help you to make thousands by avoiding the mistakes I made. In just a few days or even a few hours you can learn what it took me ten years to experience.

You may be wondering why I am giving away my success secrets. It may surprise you but there are no secrets. Thousands of people are already doing what I am about to describe. And there is room for thousands more, too.

What I am going to give you is a lot of sound advice, thoroughly tested by myself and other successful investors. This book can be your shortcut to success. You don't need to have years of experience as a real estate agent.

This book will explain the ins and outs of investing in single-family (residential) homes. It will outline a hypothetical investment program which can turn an initial $3,000 investment into as much as $300,000 equity in 11 years or less.

You will find that it is not really difficult to make a $300,000 nest egg. You don't need a big income, a lot of beginning capital, a lot of time, specialized knowledge or even good luck.

I'll show you how to use what I call the six basic "Success Factors." When you can master these six basic concepts you can be on your personal road to success.

These factors are:

1. Leverage
2. Appreciation
3. Buying
4. Maintaining your property
5. Retrieving your profits
6. Borrowing other people's money

A Word of Caution

A word of caution is in order. The many investment principles mentioned here are applicable to most communities in every state in the union. What works in Walnut Creek, California, will also work in Cincinnati or Dallas. But the facts of law referred to are only applicable to California residents. While it is true that many laws are very similar in nature and purpose from one state to another, all references are to California law. It would be impossible in a book of this nature to interpret the real estate laws of 50 states.

While I refer often to deeds of trust, which are used as an instrument to convey title, you can freely interchange the term mortgage for deed of trust as there is basically little difference between the two.

It is also not the purpose of this book to give you legal or tax advice. Described are legal situations and an explanation of basic tax concepts. When the need arises, consult your attorney or accountant.

I

Why
Single Family
Homes?

I sincerely believe that single family home investments are the surest and fastest way to make big money in real estate . . . or in any investment field. It is very common for an investor to earn 50 per cent or even 100 per cent return each year on money invested in rental homes. The profit isn't realized, of course, until the property is sold. But the profit is there for the taking. Let's examine a few other popular investment alternatives:

Stock Market: Anyone who has invested in a broad range of stocks over the past three years has probably lost a great deal of equity. The market has experienced many ups and downs. I know one investor who had stocks with a value of $35,000 in early 1972. The same portfolio was worth only $17,000 three years later, representing an $18,000 loss.

If you are an experienced and knowledgeable investor you can make money in the stock market. But for most people the stock market is a very big gamble.

Savings Accounts: I don't like to knock savings accounts. Money accumulated from savings goes into the real estate market in the form of mortgages. This conventional money market is invaluable to the real estate industry.

But facts are facts: The interest you earn on these accounts is not enough to be considered an investment. Even an 8 per cent return you would get on a long-term certificate account can be wiped out with taxes and the present rate of inflation.

Gold and Silver: Investing in gold and silver is a glamorous idea, but it is highly speculative. Gold and silver pay no dividends and you must pay storage costs or risk theft. The gold and silver market is probably subject to more ups and downs than even the stock market.

Rare Coins: I have about $500 invested in a collection because I enjoy coins as a hobby. Many coins have appreciated in value greatly over the past years. But this is one investment that should be left to the experts. And this is not my advice but the words of the coin dealer that I deal with.

Second Deeds of Trust: Seconds (which will be explained in detail in Chapter VIII) are the next best investment after single family homes. Seconds are secured by real property and can earn from 8 to 25 per cent per annum. You are limited by state usury laws as to what interest rates you can charge. In most states the limit is 10 per cent. But many investors buy "seasoned" seconds at big discounts which enable them to earn upwards of 25 per cent. The proper use of seconds will be a major factor in your single family home investment program.

Vacant Land: The most speculative and romantic real estate investment is raw land. Fortunes have been made and many are still being made. The principle sounds simple: Buy land in the path of progress and then wait five or 10 years to resell and cash in the chips.

This might work for you, too, if you can: 1. afford to set aside $20,000 or $30,000 that pays no dividends; 2. afford to pay $1,000 to $5,000 per year in taxes; and 3. have the good fortune to accurately pick a parcel of land that will be in the path of progress.

Land investments are not for everybody. You must have a lot of insight and a lot of money.

Commercial Property: Commercial property can be an individual unit or a large, multi-million-dollar investment. It's a highly specialized field that takes a lot of capital, carries high risk and should be left alone by the average investor.

Income Property: Multi-unit investment property can give you the tax shelter and profits that you will find in single family homes. However, it is a highly specialized field that takes a large amount of capital and more knowledge than you can obtain in a short period of time.

After following the program outlined in Chapter VIII, you will have the capital and experience to trade your homes for multi-unit property if you desire.

Single Family Homes: Single family home investments can be for nearly everyone. It does not take a lot of beginning capital nor does it take a lot of experience. This book is dedicated to the philosophy of single family home investing. As you read on you will understand why so many people are successfully investing in homes. Soon you will be able to play a real life game of Monopoly, not too much different from the famous Parker Brothers' game.

14 Million Investors Can't Be Wrong

Results of a Realtor-sponsored Gallup survey show that one out of every five American families own real estate other than their home; and 7.3 per cent owned another one-family residence. That means that approximately 14 million Americans own rental homes. There are many good reasons why this is so.

1. *Easiest:* Single family homes are the easiest real estate investment to buy, to manage and to sell. Only vacant land offers less management considerations. Rental homes are also subject to less governmental control than multi-unit apartments. And I've yet to hear about an organized rent strike harassing single-family home landlords.

2. *Appreciation and Yield:* We'll go into this subject a lot more later in the book. It is appreciation to a large degree that helps you bring in yearly yields of 25 . . . 50 . . . 75 . . . and even 100 per cent on your invested dollar.

3. *Safety:* There is an old stock market maxim which goes something like this: A conservative buyer should buy into a company that sells a product which will always be in demand — like a utility. This same principle is what makes real estate — particularly homes — a very sound and safe investment. People will always require shelter.

4. *Liquidity:* Real estate is just as liquid as any other investment. And single family homes are more liquid (principle of converting your properties into ready cash) than any other type of real estate investment. Priced realistically, your real property can be sold quickly at a fair market price. This is a determining liquidity factor in any investment.

   When the stock market is in one of its many slumps, you can sell and receive your funds within a few days. But you can't call that good liquidity when you have to take a big loss to sell. You'll never have to wait a year or so for prices to return to their original levels in the real estate market.

   A big advantage of single family homes over multi-unit property is the liquidity of just a small part of your investment.

   For example, let's say that one investor owns five homes with a combined equity of $100,000. The second investor owns a 10-unit apartment with an equity of $100,000. If either investor needs $20,000 cash, which one do you think would come out best? The second investor would have only two real choices: He would have to sell his entire apartment complex or he would have to take out a costly second loan.

The single family home investor would also have two choices. He would have to take out a second loan on one or possibly two of his properties or he could sell just one of the homes. Therein lies the advantage. The owner of the single family homes can "peel off" just one of his investments and keep the others working for him.

5. *Tax Shield:* What other investment can give you both a tax shield and a huge profit on your investment? And with each single family home being a separate entity with its own tax base, you can maneuver properties as in a chess match to give you almost any desired effect — like a lot of tax-free income in a poor income year or a lot of tax shield when you need it most. It doesn't take many properties to put a lot of investors in a position where they can legally avoid state and federal income taxes. A lot more will be said about tax shelters later on.

6. *Scarcity:* In 1976 the last of the American-made convertibles were sold by Cadillac. Later the same year any owner of a 1976 Cadillac convertible could have sold his car for double the money he paid for it. Why? The answer is simple! Cadillac convertibles — as well as other makes of convertibles — became so scarce that they were worth a premium price.

The very same thing is happening to homes. The inexpensive single family home is not being built fast enough in most communities to meet consumer demands. In fact, in many parts of the country THE INEXPENSIVE HOME IS NOT EVEN BEING BUILT AT ALL as builders continue to construct larger (and more expensive) models that return a greater profit. And often the blame belongs not to the builders but to the government, which continues to demand more and more building requirements which in turn are added to the price of the home.

The net result is that few new homes are being built that low-to-moderate income families can afford to buy. But the demand from both tenants and first-home buyers for inexpensive property grows stronger each day, thus helping to push prices ever upwards. Needless to say, this situation creates many opportunities for investors.

7. *Less Expensive to Buy:* The single family home costs the investor less to buy than vacant land, commercial real estate or multi-family property. In most areas of the country an investor can get going with less than $4,000 and even in the highest priced areas an investor can still get by for less than $12,000. This means that a single family home investor can pyramid his holdings more quickly into a small real estate empire.

8. *Higher Occupancy Rates:* All of the previously described advantages of single family homes can be summed up in one word . . . *DEMAND.* People must have a roof over their heads! And survey after survey has shown that buyers and tenants alike consider the most desirable shelter to be the single family home.

    Because of this demand, the traditional vacancy rates for the single-unit home are negligible. Recent government surveys show that the vacancy rates for single family homes are always lower than for multi-family property. According to the U.S. Census Bureau's quarterly household surveys, for example, "for rent" vacancies of single family homes in Seattle (1976) amounted to only 1.7 per cent as compared to 4.8 per cent for apartments. In Miami the figures read 1.1 per cent for homes and 5.6 per cent for multi-units. The story was basically the same in every major U.S. housing market.

II

Getting Started

The beauty of a single family home investment portfolio is that you don't need a lot of money or a big income to get started.

If you have $3,000 in the bank and if you can afford to set aside up to $100.00 each month, then you may be financially ready to start on a rewarding 11-year journey that can increase your net worth by as much as $300,000. You don't need a big income, either. Many investors I know have annual incomes of only $12,000 per year.

The very best way to start your real estate investment program is to buy your own home. It's the best investment you'll ever make!

After our second child was born, my wife and I sold our two-bedroom home and bought a larger four-bedroom split-level for $50,000. That was in mid-1971. Five years later my home was worth more than $76,000. My mortgage payment including taxes and insurance is just under $400. Just think! In five years I paid about $24,000 in house payments, and during the same period my value increased by about $26,000 plus another $2,500 in loan paydown. And the home brought more than $4,000 a year in tax deductions, which saved me another $1,000 per year. Applying my tax savings to needed repairs and improvements, I came out with better than a free residence for five years.

Yes, I strongly recommend buying your own home. But it is not necessary, however, as you can rent an apartment and follow my principles and still have a very successful investment portfolio. For most people, though, owning their home is the first step. When you are a homeowner, you get your biggest tax break from Uncle Sam — and this means that you will have more money available to spend and thus invest in rental properties. Being a homeowner also means that you will have established credit and a source for borrowing.

There Is More Than One Way To Skin A Cat

I have stated that you are ready to begin investing if you have $3,000 to spend and if you can afford another $100 per month. Breaking those figures down, the $3,000 is for your down payment and closing costs on your first purchase. Fifty dollars of the $100 is to be saved monthly for a second purchase two years after your first. The remaining $50 is an estimate of what you may need to cover either repairs or negative cashflows, which are covered in greater detail in Chapters IV and V.

If you are able and willing to perform all maintenance chores on your rentals, you can save a fair amount of money. I am not personally able or willing to "fix and paint." I don't have the time, for one thing, and besides, I am all thumbs. I found out that it does not make that much difference in the long run. As you read on, I think you will see what I mean.

You can reach $300,000 in equities much faster than the hypothetical program outlined in Chapter VIII, if you are willing to start out with more than $3,000. There is more than one way to skin a cat! Here are four ways you can start out with more money and more properties.

- The first method is the obvious. If you have $10,000 or $20,000 to invest, then go ahead and do so. You will be far ahead of most and on a shorter time table.

- If you do not have $3,000 but have owned your home for enough time to build up a respectable equity, then borrow. By means of a second deed of trust you can borrow as much as $3,000 to $10,000. The extra costs incurred by the second will be worth it in the long run.

- See your friendly banker. If you do not have enough equity in your home for a second, check out your bank. With good credit and references you can borrow enough money from the bank to start your investment program or even buy a second property. I have used this method twice to buy property that was too good a bargain to pass up.

- Borrow from relatives. Your best terms can often be arranged with understanding relatives. Several years ago I borrowed $3,000 from my father to purchase a home. I am paying back interest only at $25 per month for an indefinite period of time. That $3,000, incidentally, stands behind two homes now with combined equities of over $25,000.

Save For A Year?

If you can save $225 a month for one year and at the same time earn 5 per cent interest, you will have accumulated about $3,000 for your first purchase. *But don't be fooled by this method!* As you will see later in the book, homes will appreciate in value at a far greater rate than 5 per cent per year.

The best advice I can give you is not to put off buying. Borrow rather than save! This might sound like strange advice — but borrowing is saving in the long run. For instance, let's assume that you can buy a three-bedroom home for $30,000 with a $3,000 down payment. But you don't have the money unless you borrow from a finance company that charges a $500 loan fee plus 10 per cent interest for a term of three years. The grand total on $3,500 comes to $112.95 per month for three years.

But here is the corker. The home you buy today for $30,000 will most likely be worth $33,000 one year from now. If you wait a year while you save money for your down payment, you will lose big.

Don't put off until tomorrow what you can do today! If you have a way to borrow and can handle the monthly payments then do so. Start yourself on the road to tax savings and equity growth now. I've never known anyone who has made money in real estate by *waiting* for the right time to buy.

When It Costs More To Buy

Unfortunately, everything is not always equal. Many parts of the country have experienced wild increases in home values — especially since 1975. In these high-priced areas — such as the Washington, D.C. vicinity and most suburban areas of California — it is almost impossible for an investor to find good rental property buys that take less than a $10,000 outlay.

Even though the leverage is not as good, investors in these high-priced areas can still make a substantial profit — in many cases even a greater profit than investors in low-priced areas. This happens when home values increase at a faster rate — often 15 per cent or more — than in slower appreciating areas where the gain might be less than 10 per cent.

The only major disadvantage for investors in high priced areas is that it takes more cash to buy a property. Thus they may not be able to buy homes at as fast a rate as the investors in lower-priced areas.

There are two basic reasons why an investor's initial outlay can quickly jump from $3,000 to $10,000. The first reason is obvious — it takes a bigger down payment in most circumstances to buy a $60,000 home than it does to purchase a $30,000 property.

The second reason may not seem so obvious at first. In communities where the medium-priced home is less than $40,000 there will be a substantial number of homes purchased with new FHA or GI loans. As I point out later on, upon resale these FHA or GI loans can offer tremendous advantages to the investor seeking to pay as little down payment as possible when buying.

In areas where the medium-priced home is a lot higher (like $60,000 or more) you will find very few homes being bought with FHA or GI loans. Homes in this price range are in a conventional loan market and in this type of a market you will find very few sellers who are willing to pay loan discount points so that a buyer can arrange FHA or GI financing. The net result is that the investors' supply of *resale assumptions* with low down payments is very limited. They are not impossible to find, I might add, but difficult. But this situation may dramatically change!

A Prediction for 1978

In October, 1977, Congress passed a new law which increased the maximum amount of an FHA loan from $45,000 to $60,000. And at the same time they greatly liberalized the minimum down payment requirement so that a buyer may now purchase a $60,000 home with only $2,500 down plus closing costs. The new down payment schedule is three per cent down on the first $25,000 and five per cent down on the remaining balance to a maximum of $60,000.

The result of this new law will be a substantially higher number of new FHA and GI sales, especially during 1978 and early '79. This is turn will give investors a better crack at low down payment assumption buys in both high- and low-priced communities.

III

Leverage and Appreciation

Let your imagination run wild for a moment! Imagine that you and I each inherited $100,000 from a long-lost relative. I'll take mine and buy three rental homes — with cash. No loans whatsoever. And each home will rent for $300 a month so after taxes and upkeep I will come out with $200 per home or a grand total of $600. Not bad! In 10 years I'll have pocketed $72,000 in rent proceeds plus if my three homes go up in value by 10 per cent per year they will be worth a staggering $260,000.

Well, you are no dummy either! But you take a different approach. You don't buy just three homes, but 15. However, you have a loan against each property and because your mortgage payments plus taxes, insurance and upkeep come to more than $300 per month . . . you have to "feed" your investments $25 each or $375 each month out of your own pocket. So after 10 years I've pocketed $72,000 and you've lost $45,000. Okay, now figure out what is the financial genius . . . you or me.

You are — and by a landslide. I have accumulated $260,000 (three homes without a mortgage) plus $72,000 minus about $25,000 that I had to pay in income taxes for a grand total of $307,000.

But you . . . now that is a different story. You own 15 homes with mortgages (but the principal amount of each loan has been reduced $3,000 during the 10 years) and the total value of your 15 homes is now $1,300,000. After 10 years each of your loans would be about $25,000 or $375,000 for all 15 properties. Subtracting the loans from the total value of the homes you now have $925,000 to my $307,000.

But one more thing must be subtracted from your total — and that is the $45,000 you had to feed the homes during the 10 years. BUT HOLD EVERYTHING! You would have had an excellent tax shelter where I would not have had any. In fact you had enough shelter to protect almost your entire salary. So you really didn't lose $45,000.

Back to reality. What I demonstrated was how LEVERAGE, the first of six essential SUCCESS FACTORS, is so vital if you want to make really big money with a rental home program. The use of leverage is simple but extremely important to your success.

Leverage means controlling a $1 product for a dime and then later selling the product for $2. You make a clear $1 profit while only risking one thin dime. That comes to a resounding 1,000 per cent profit. Now if you paid out $1 for the $1 product and then sold it for $2 you would have made a nice, but comparatively small 100 per cent return. Smart investors — in any field — always use leverage.

In real estate, leverage simply means controlling the most property with the least amount of money. The greater your skill in using leverage, the greater will be the return on your dollar. As you read on, you will clearly see how this principle will create wealth for you almost overnight.

Understanding Inflation

"An average *NEW* single family home similar to the one you could have bought for $24,600 in 1967, costs $52,300 today," according to a news release by the U.S. Commerce Department.

That's more than a 100 per cent increase in 10 years.

Rising prices caused by inflation can certainly be a serious problem for the consumer. But to the real estate investor, inflation can be an ally. And that is because real estate — so very sensitive to inflation — historically keeps right up with rising prices.

Every time a carpenter or a bricklayer receives a new contract for higher wages the price of new homes goes up a notch. And just like the shadow that follows your body, the prices of used homes follow right along.

The second success factor is APPRECIATION. Appreciation and inflation go hand in hand. You cannot have inflation without real property appreciating (going up) in value. To be successful . . . you must believe this. You must anticipate inflation and appreciating values. The government does! All long-range government planning takes inflation into consideration.

Here are some more startling figures: "Less than 23 years from now, a senior airline pilot will be paid $292,500 a year. That is good news — for him. Here is the bad. If he lives in Duchess County, N.Y., his new kitchen cabinet will be installed by a carpenter who makes $128,200. Or, if home sweet home is in San Francisco, his leaky faucet will be fixed by a plumber who makes $137,200."

Those are the projections of Manplan Consultants, a Chicago-headquartered management consulting firm. Their figures are based on past wage trends, plus the effect of inflation. Manplan also predicts that the minimum wage should be at least $19,800 by the year 2000 and that a job paying an annual salary of $25,000 in 1975 will be paying $112,500 in the year 2000.

It's not very pleasant to contemplate, but if you have a one-year-old child whom you plan to send to a four-year university in the 1990's it will cost $47,330 at a state school and $82,830 at a private one. The figures were compiled by the Oakland Financial Group of Charlottesville, Va., which based its estimate of future college costs on an annual inflation rate of 6 per cent and included tuition, room, board, travel, books and incidentals.

When your money is invested in real estate you will have more than a hedge against inflation. You will have an investment that—in most years—will keep you AHEAD of inflation.

Using Inflation—To Your Advantage

If you bury your money in a tin can it is obvious that inflation will rob you. But it should also be obvious that many other investments do not bring a high enough return to even keep up with the cost of living index in most years, notably savings accounts and many stocks.

Below are recent Cost-of-Living Index Figures (also known as the Consumer Price Index) as compiled by the U.S. Department of Labor. The index is based on a sampling of some 400 items and serves as an indicator of price trends for food, clothing, housing, health care, transportation and recreation. Check the figures against your current investments. Are you keeping up?

1974	12.2%
1975	7.0%
1976	4.8%
1977*	6.6%
Less than 4-year inflation rate	30.6%

The figures for 1977 are incomplete as they are only through Sept.

Now during this same time span look what has happened to the average prices of single family homes.

	June 1974	June 1977
Western region	$35,420	$58,100
Northeast region	$36,530	$45,100
Southern region	$33,050	$40,500
North Central region	$28,180	$37,200

If present trends continue, according to a recent joint study by Harvard University and M.I.T., the average NEW home, which sells for $52,300 in early 1977, will go for $78,000 by 1981.

I am not attempting to justify inflation but rather to show how it can be used to help make you money. A steady rate of inflation between 5 and 8 per cent is a healthy factor from a real estate standpoint. Combining inflation rates of 8 to 12 per cent with the principle of leverage can reap excellent profits for an investor. But when many homes appreciate at over 20 per cent, as happened in California during 1976 and early 1977, it is not a good thing because a short cooling-off period is bound to follow. Steady growth is the best.

Even though I told you that with high inflation rates you can reap big profits, you must not solely base an investment program on rising costs. Rental homes can be profitable investments at even zero appreciation. Buying and selling correctly, combined with good leverage, will still make you money. Inflation only sweetens the pot a little as you can buy more homes on a faster time schedule.

Pressures That Increase Appreciation

More often than not real property appreciates at a faster rate than the Cost-of-Living Index increases. There are many reasons why this is so. I've already discussed the everyday variety of inflation, which is primarily caused by wage increases. Here are four more reasons why homes prices in most communities will continue to soar:

1. **Post Korean War baby boom:** The last big U.S. baby boom, that of the post-Korean War period, is beginning to enter the job market. For the next decade, approximately 2.5 million persons will enter the labor force for the first time each year, swelling the 20- to 34-year-old age group from 40 million in 1968 to over 68 million by 1980. The net results of this phenomenon is an increased demand for inexpensive homes.

2. **Increasing population:** You have heard all the talk about smaller families, etc. But don't be fooled. Our population is still growing fast. Consider that every 9 seconds there is a birth in the United States. Every 16½ seconds there is a death. Every 60 seconds an immigrant arrives. Every 23 minutes a U.S. resident departs to live in another country. The net result is an addition of one person to the U.S. population every 15½ seconds, four every minute, more than 232 every hour and more than 5,575 every day. The upshot—even more housing pressure.

3. **More working wives:** More wives are working now—and they are making more money than ever. More than half of the nation's 47.3 million husband-wife families had more than one wage earner, according to a Labor Department survey. And with new credit laws in effect, the wife's income is now fully accepted in qualifying for new mortgage payments. The effect—still more housing pressure.

4. **Building problems:** As you can readily see, there is a lot of pressure for housing in this country. Demand for new housing will be higher in the next ten years than ever before. But at today's production levels we are falling far short of meeting that demand.

New housing starts spurt and sputter. When interest rates are low or at least reasonable, then new building starts begin to reach the needed level. But when interest rates jump too high, as in 1974, then new housing starts don't even approach the needed levels.

"New housing starts, including mobile home deliveries, are now running at an annualized rate of approximately 1.6 million, but more are needed," according to Don W. Carlson, Chairman of the Board of Consolidated Capital Equities Corp. in Oakland, California.

Carlson goes on to say that "there is already a shortfall of approximately 400,000 units a year. Moreover, we forecast that, during the next 10 years, at least 2.2 million new shelter units will be required each year to satisfy the net demand resulting from increases in family units and obsolescence."

What does this mean? More pressure from both first-home buyers and tenants.

Who Can Afford To Buy Homes?

If you have kept your eyes and ears open lately, I know that you've heard a lot about the "affordability of homes." Some say that we are headed for trouble because soon nobody will be able to buy homes. I disagree!

Don't forget the pilot that is supposed to make $292,500 by the year 2000. Besides, despite high prices, new government figures

(U.S. Department of Commerce) show that people in nearly all states are making more money now. It reports that the average income of every man, woman and child in the U.S. in 1976 rose 9 per cent from the previous year.

Here are samples of some of the state-wide figures:

Arizona	Up 9.4%
California	Up 8.6%
District of Columbia	Up 11.6%
Louisiana	Up 10.0%
Michigan	Up 13.4%
Missouri	Up 9.4%
Oregon	Up 10.1%
Texas	Up 10.8%
Vermont	Up 10.4%

Only two states — North and South Dakota — showed a decline.

Despite pessimistic talk by "inflation worriers," the National Association of Realtors announced that in October, 1977, the seasonally adjusted annual rate of home sales reached a peak of 3,930,000 units — a figure which already tops the full-year record total of 3,002,000 sales set in 1976.

There is a lesson to be learned here: Do not be afraid to buy real estate — even at today's record high prices — because you don't think anyone will be able to afford to buy it later on. If you think like that, you will never be a financial winner.

Who can afford to buy homes? Obviously a lot of people! In today's economy the question should be: Who can afford NOT to buy homes? U.S. News & World Report, in their January 16, 1978, issue, compared the ability of eight popular investments to beat inflation . . . not just keep up but stay ahead of it over a five-year period.

Only one of the eight was able to beat inflation. It wasn't the stock market . . . the study showed that money invested there ($10,000) actually decreased to $9,580. The second best investment (for a person in the 25 per cent tax bracket) was certificate of deposits which showed that $10,000 would add up to $13,136 in a five-year span.

The best investment for keeping ahead of inflation? You guessed it. The everyday variety of dwelling called the HOME. According to U.S. News & World Report, an investment of $10,000 would have to end up being worth $14,570 just to stay even with inflation. A single family home investment of $10,000 was worth $18,901 to a person in the 25 per cent tax bracket and $21,140 to someone in a 42 per cent bracket.

The following chart reaffirms that both prices and wages pretty much stay even with each other.

WAGE STATISTICS
BASED UPON LABOR DEPARTMENT'S
CONSUMER PRICE INDEX

	1965 $2.45/hour	1970 $3.22/hour	1974 $4.25/hour
1 lb. hamburger	13 min.	13 min.	14 min.
1 doz. eggs	13 min.	11 min.	11 min.
1 quart milk	6 min.	6 min.	5 min.
1 pr. men's shoes	6 hr. 7 min.	6 hrs.	5 hr. 44 min.
1 man's shirt	4 hr. 5 min.	3 hr. 32 min.	3 hr. 5 min.
sgl-family home	12,224 hr. 54 min.	12,909 hr. 19 min.	12,783 hr. 32 min.
refrigerator	65 hr. 18 min.	50 hr. 26 min.	42 hr. 48 min.
electricity bill	4 hr. 5 min.	3 hr. 26 min.	3 hr. 38 min.
property tax	40 hr. 49 min.	41 hr. 4 min.	38 hr. 43 min.
new automobile	816 hr. 20 min.	662 hr. 20 min.	552 hr.
1 gal. gasoline	8 min.	7 min.	8 min.
bicycle	20 hr. 25 min.	17 hr. 33 min.	16 hr. 57 min.
hrly parking fee	37 min.	42 min.	36 min.
airline fare	40 hr. 49 min.	36 hr. 55 min.	34 hr. 59 min.
television set	122 hr. 27 min.	86 hr. 39 min.	65 hr. 35 min.
movie admission	37 min.	42 min.	39 min.
basketball	4 hr. 5 min.	3 hr. 44 min.	3 hr. 20 min.
1 can dog food	6 min.	5 min.	5 min.
magazine subsc.	2 hr. 52 min.	2 hr. 43 min.	2 hr. 28 min.
hospital room (semi-private)	12 hr. 14 min.	17 hr. 50 min.	19 hr. 30 min.
tonsillectomy	61 hr. 22 min.	59 hr. 56 min.	57 hr. 59 min.
funeral	408 hr. 10 min.	366 hr. 49 min.	336 hr.
cigar	12 min.	13 min.	11 min.
6-pack beer	29 min.	26 min.	24 min.
short-form will	20 hr. 25 min.	20 hr. 58 min.	22 hr. 45 min.

IV

Buying
Rental Properties

Several years ago I spotted an ad in my local newspaper for a two-bedroom home for $21,000. I called the owner, who was selling the property himself, and identified myself as Dave Glubetich, Realtor. I was told—and not too politely—that not only was I not needed, I was most unwelcome.

Two weeks later I spotted another "For-Sale-By-Owner" ad for a two-bedroom home. This time the price was $14,600. I called, since this price was the lowest for any home that I had seen in Pleasant Hill for a couple of years.

I was shocked when I discovered that this was the same home—the same owner—that I had talked with two weeks earlier. I jumped in my car and was at his home in less than 10 minutes. I told the owner that I wanted to buy his home. Now! Not a minute later!

This anxious seller was mad at the world. He didn't like high taxes and he didn't like California. He wanted to sell fast—so fast that he insisted the buyer not have any contingencies in the contract, including the usual "subject to buyer and property qualifying for a new loan."

There I was, faced with perhaps the best opportunity that I had ever seen. There was no doubt in my mind that his two-bedroom home had a value of at least $21,000. But I did not have $14,600 which, incidentally, was the official assessed value of the property. I wanted to use the time-honored principle of leverage.

As I sat there discussing the terms with the owner, he must have received at least five phone calls about the home. Who could pass up an opportunity to check out a steal like this? But to my complete amazement all of the callers backed down when they discovered the home had slab floors rather than hardwood floors. It made no difference in the value. It made no difference to an investor. It was an excellent home in a better than average neighborhood and this same home in 1977 would sell for $52,000.

Well, I recognized the value and I was going to buy the home one way or another. What I did was arrange a short-term loan from my banker for the $14,600 plus closing costs. I had to put up everything I owned as collateral but it was worth it. Because I knew that once I bought the home I could then refinance it or sell it for a tremendous short-term profit.

This brings us to the third success factor, which is BUYING. The three vital elements of *buying* are location, condition and financing. When buying property, you will always be more successful if you will bring along a little common sense and a dose of flexibility. In the above example, I would have been the big loser if I had not been flexible in my ideas about financing.

Location

The location of a property is all-important for our purposes. One of the first things an appraising student learns is that "location, location, location" are the three most important factors in determining real property values. In the same community two identical homes can have as much as a $5,000 difference in value because of different locations.

You must always be aware of location. But don't become obsessed with it because it is also true that other factors enter the picture. For instance a home in a not too desirable neighborhood will possibly appreciate in value at the same rate as the home in a better neighborhood. And the homes in the best neighborhood may not lend themselves to rental investments because of price or a lack of assumable FHA and GI loans.

Don't equate location with price range either. A good location can be a subdivision that is generally well kept and not in any immediate danger from encroaching commercial or multiple zoning changes. Price range is relatively unimportant. A neighborhood of $25,000 homes can be just as good a location as an area of $50,000 homes.

You must think of resale values four or five years down the road. Thus you need a property and neighborhood that will be attractive in the foreseeable future. Do not purchase property that backs up to a freeway, shopping center or a multi-story bulding. To a large degree it is location that you will soon be selling. And a poor location will cost you money.

Condition

The condition of the home you buy is very important. The property you buy should be clean, freshly painted, in good repair, well landscaped and have a relatively new roof.

It should be obvious what a home in top-flight condition will do for you. It will mean that you will not have immediate repair bills. It will also help attract the best tenants who will pay you top rental dollars for the home. And with excellent tenants your property will be better kept over the years and your profits can be maximized.

Avoid properties that are extremely run down, or ones that have major structural problems or are in immediate need of a new roof. This type of property should only be purchased if the price is rock bottom low. Also avoid homes that do not have a garage, are over 30 years old or have outmoded heating systems.

Your best bet is a property that has been owner-occupied and shows a lot of love and care. With this type of property you won't have to spend a penny prior to selecting your first tenant.

Financing

To effectively use the principle of leverage you must pay down as little money as possible. The very best way to do this is to assume an FHA or GI loan. These loans are government insured and any buyer can take over an FHA or GI loan without qualification or without any changes or increases in the interest rates. Also there is no prepayment charge on these loans.

At this writing, most conventional loans are currently being made at interest rates from 8½ to 9½ per cent. A conventional loan, incidentally, is a loan not insured directly by the U.S. Government. You cannot assume these loans at their stated rate, because the lender can—and will—raise the interest to the current rate.

An exception to the above statements would be some loans under the auspices of the Federal National Mortgage Association (Fannie Mae). They are low down payment conventional loans with private mortgage insurance. Some of these loans can be assumed at their present interest rates and with no prepayment charge. Rather than get into a technical discussion of the hows and whys, I suggest you always check with your Realtor or the lender involved when you are faced with a Fannie Mae loan.

In Contra Costa County, where I have my office, there are not as many FHA and GI loan assumptions available as there once were.

The reason is simple—prices are high. My city (Pleasant Hill) averaged $58,000 in January, 1977, vs. $43,000 in nearby Sacramento.

Whereas many $5,000 FHA and GI assumptions are available in Sacramento, you have to look far and wide now to find any for even $10,000 in the Pleasant Hill area. But it is important to remember that even in high price areas your investment program can be just as successful as in lower-priced areas. What you must do is shift your emphasis from government loan assumptions to conventional loans with secondary financing.

New Conventional Loans

"When all else fails—take a different road." The time will probably come when you will find the perfect home in all respects except one . . . the loan will not be assumable or the balance will be too low and thus take too much cash.

This has happened to me more than once. And my answer to the problem has been to purchase the property with a new conventional loan. Many savings and loans will welcome investor buyers as long as the loan is no less than 80 per cent of their appraised value. They will also allow the seller to take back a second deed of trust in the amount of 10 per cent.

One such purchase was four years ago when I paid $28,000 for a four-bedroom home. I paid $2,800 (10 per cent) down and had the seller carry back a $2,800 (10 per cent) second at 10 per cent interest only payments for a term of five years. The seller also paid all of my closing costs for the new loan so that my actual cost was only $2,800. Today, I estimate the value of this home to be $55,000. Not bad leverage and profit in just four years, considering that I didn't assume an FHA or GI loan.

There are some disadvantages in using conventional financing for your investment portfolio. But you can overcome many of these problems.

1. *Higher closing costs:* With a purchase price of $30,000, your conventional closing costs would be approximately 4 per cent or $1,200 in most communities. Your assumption closing costs would be a lot less. You can minimize this problem by having the seller pay at least half of the closing costs. Most lenders will allow this but you might have to shop around if the first one says no.

2. *Qualification:* There are absolutely no qualification requirements to assume an FHA or GI loan whereas you will be sub-

ject to close scrutiny by the conventional lender. If you have good credit, job history and income—there will be no problem. This is not as difficult as it may sound. The lender realizes that your rental property produces income so he isn't looking for a super qualified buyer.

3. *Pre-Payment Penalties:* Prepayment penalties can be high on conventional loans—often six months' interest. This can often be waived upon resale if the new buyer refinances through the same lender.

4. *Interest rates:* The only real disadvantage with conventional loans is that they cannot be assumed at current rates like FHA and GI's. However, new development in the field of variable interest rate mortgages is changing this picture some. A full explanation is in Chapter IX.

5. *Leverage:* Your leverage can be just as good with conventional loans if you pay no more than 10 per cent down. Because no lender that I know of will knowingly let an investor buy a rental property with just 10 per cent down, you must obtain an 80 per cent loan. To keep the kind of leverage you need for a fast-growing equity portfolio, you will need to have the seller or an outside source take back a 10 per cent second. And to keep your total payments and cash flow loss to a minimum you will have to obtain the second at interest only payments.

The above works. You might have to make three or four offers on different property to get just the terms you want, but you will find that conventional loan buying will open more doors.

GI Loans

Assuming an FHA loan presents very few problems. But the Veterans Administration loans present some considerations which the investor should be aware of.

The VA now allows a veteran to purchase a subsequent home with a "no down payment" GI loan provided that his original loan is completely paid off. This means that the vet cannot allow his loan to be assumed if he plans to buy another home for his maximum entitlement allowed. The vet loan must be paid off completely.

As bad as this might sound for the investor, all is not lost. There are three reasons why you will seldom be faced by the GI seller who will want his loan paid off.

First of all, many sellers will have no plans to purchase another home. Secondly, many of the GI's will be making their second purchase with conventional financing. The third reason is more complex, but very important for our purposes. It involves an increased maximum home loan guaranty allowed by the new Veterans Housing Act of 1974.

The new law allows the government to guarantee (the lender who makes the loan) GI loans to a maximum of $17,500. Using a formula of four times the guarantee, a veteran can purchase a home for $70,000 without a down payment. The old guarantee (also known as the veteran's entitlement) level was $12,500. That level was in effect from May 1, 1968, to December 31, 1974. Prior to that time the level was $7,500.

Using this guideline, a vet who bought a home in 1972 under the $12,500 guarantee level will have an additional $5,000 entitlement remaining to buy a second home. This means he can buy a home for $20,000 (4 × $5,000) without any down payment. If the vet is buying a $40,000 property he will need to make a down payment of only $4,000 which represents 20 per cent of the total above his remaining entitlement of $20,000. Thus the new rules help make it possible for the GI seller to allow his loan to be assumed.

The new VA Housing Act of 1974 also gives a break to the GI homeowner who would like to refinance and invest the extra dollars in rental property. With all GI homeowners affected by the increased entitlement, the vet can now refinance and use the extra money for any purpose. The vet can even keep his original home for a rental property and use his increased entitlement to purchase a new residence.

A word of warning: If you are ever in a position where you can assume a new GI loan, make sure that the property was held by the vet for at least one month. Uncle Sam works in slow and mysterious ways so it usually takes three to four weeks after close of escrow before a lender receives the official VA guarantee. If title passes too quickly it could jeopardize the loan.

Three More Ways To Buy

Up to this point, I have suggested buying rental properties by either assuming FHA or GI loans or refinancing with conventional terms. Most of your investments will utilize these methods.

As an investor, however, you should be aware of other excellent alternatives which you might some day be able to use. All of these alternative methods involve the seller taking part in the financing. Therefore it is necessary to find a seller who would rather have a monthly income than a large sum of money. The three techniques are: contract of sale; overriding deed of trust; and purchase money mortgage.

A **contract of sale** (or land contract) is seldom used in California but quite popular in most areas of the country. It can be quite useful when a seller has either no outstanding loan or a very small balance against his property. Under this type of contract, the seller retains the title in his name. A down payment from 10 to 20 per cent should enable you to make a purchase via a contract of sale, but be sure and check with your Realtor regarding local custom and state laws.

The second method, **purchase money mortgage**, is more common than you might realize. It can be used in a situation like the contract of sale, where the seller has little or no loan and carries the entire amount after a reasonable down payment. With the seller being in the lender's position he is able to earn better interest rates than a bank or savings institution would pay. And the buyer saves also because he will usually escape loan fees and prepayment charges. A title or escrow company will be more than happy to properly prepare the required mortgage papers.

An **overriding deed of trust**, can be described for our purposes as a method of conveying property in which the buyer takes title by assuming the original loan and the seller advances the buyer the difference between the first loan and the amount being financed. For an "overriding" to work the first loan must be assumable without any escalation of interest. Thus an FHA or GI loan is ideal.

It works this way: On a $30,000 sale the buyer makes a $3,000 (10 per cent) down payment and finances $27,000 which includes the original loan ($15,000) and the $12,000 difference between the first loan and $27,000. Because the seller has a $12,000 stake in the property he charges the buyer one interest rate for the full $27,000 package. Thus if the first loan is at 6 per cent and the seller charges 8½ per cent, he makes 2½ per cent profit on the $15,000 first loan and 8½ per cent profit on the $12,000 second loan. The buyer makes only one monthly payment which covers both sections of the loan.

As in the previous two methods, both buyer and seller can make out quite well because of the elimination of pre-payment penalties and loan fees. The only ingredient necessary is a seller that does not need all of his equity and is willing to settle for a good return on his money for a period of years. Perhaps for tax purposes the seller doesn't want all his money now. These methods can be complicated so be sure and use the guidance of your Realtor who will in turn rely upon legal and title company advice.

The Price Is Secondary

The price you pay for your rental home is relatively unimportant as long as it does not deviate too much from the approximate market value of the home. Market value is the highest price which a property will bring after exposed for sale in the open market. Market value can be easily determined in a subdivision with many similar homes by comparing recent sales of three properties that are a lot like the one you are considering selling or buying. For instance, if the three homes sold within a few months for prices of $32,000; $32,500 and $33,000 you can safely assume the market value to be approximately $32,500 to $33,000.

I am not advising you to go out and buy a house at any price. But I am telling you that location, condition and financing terms are more important than the eventual price you pay. (In later chapters I will discuss alternate ways to purchase property where the price is more important.)

If you can find a good buy for only $2,500 down with a low interest GI loan, then nothing else matters much. The home might be $1,000 over market value—but go ahead and buy it because appreciation (inflation) will bring the value up in perhaps as little as five or six months.

In the early stages of my real estate career I saw many sales fall apart because buyer and seller could not come to terms over as little as $200. Some of those same homes are now selling for as much as $25,000 higher in just six or seven years. It makes the $200 seem like chicken feed.

If you don't heed my recommendations, however, and you buy a home that is run-down or backs to a freeway, then you better make sure your purchase price is considerably below market value.

Down Payment

The total acquisition cost (down payment plus closing costs) is often more important than the price you pay for a property. The higher the selling price of a property the more money you will need to pay down. But whether you buy conventional or assumption, you should try to pay 10 per cent but never more than 20 per cent. In other words a $30,000 home should cost you between $3,000 and $6,000 and a $50,000 home between $5,000 and $10,000.

Your best bet for a low cash output is an FHA or GI assumption on a property in the $30,000 price range—if your area is fortunate to have any homes at this price left today. In this price range you should find many $3,000 to $4,000 assumptions because of two facts. First of all, GI buyers may buy "no down" and FHA buyers need only a $1,500 down payment on a $40,000 purchase. So any resales after just a year or less should mean a low assumption for the investor buyer.

Cash Flow

Sound easy? It is so far —even though at this stage of the book I have left out discussions of slightly more perplexing problems. We'll get into those topics later. At this point it is essential to not get bogged down, as many would-be investors do, with relatively unimportant details that can cloud your thinking and stop you from making really big profits. One such self-destructive detail is cash flow.

Positive cash flow is the amount of spendable cash you have left over from the rent income after you make your mortgage payment. Positive cash flow is a nice thing to have. It can go toward the needed repairs on the home or it can be used to take you and your wife out to dinner once a month. BUT CASH FLOW IS UNIMPORTANT! In most communities, nine out of ten times the house you purchase with a minimum down payment will have a NEGATIVE cash flow. If this prospect scares you off, then you really can't afford to invest in rental property.

In high-priced areas where home prices are appreciating better than 15 per cent a year, you can expect a negative cash flow anywhere from "0" to $100 per month. In the areas experiencing a slower appreciation rate, the cash flow will range from a $25 positive all the way to a $50 negative cash flow.

The cash flow level of your property will not remain static, however. Each year you should be able to narrow the gap until you eventually have a positive cash flow. You will be able to raise your rents from $10 to $40 each year so you will not only keep ahead of tax increases but eventually erase your negative cash flow. In 1976, for example, I was able to increase the rent on one home by $75 when a lease was signed with new tenants.

The negative cash flow problem will run in cycles. It has a lot to do with supply and demand. You have a much better chance of having a positive cash flow (or at least a *small* negative) when the demand for rental units is very strong in your community. But if a big building spurt comes along and many new apartments as well as homes are built then you will see the positive slip to a negative.

If you are on a monthly budget and a huge negative cash flow becomes a major problem, then there is an adjustment you can make: give up leveraging. By paying a higher down payment you can eliminate the uncertainties of negative cash flow. After all— isn't it better to own some rental property rather than none at all? You will still make good money, although not as much or as fast as the person who can always afford to leverage.

To understand how negative cash flow might affect your rental portfolio, you must confer with your local Realtor. The situation is different in every community, even with two adjoining cities in the same state.

Contract Terms

When buying or selling, the terms of your contract can be very important. Don't leave anything to chance—make sure that all terms and conditions ARE IN WRITING. Most states do not recognize verbal agreements in real estate matters. Following are some of the most important contract terms you will need to be familiar with when buying property.

1. *CONSIDERATION DEPOSIT*
    It is only fair to put up a healthy deposit. $500 is acceptable but $1,000 is better. But do not give the deposit directly to the seller. If you are buying through your Realtor, then have the deposit placed in his trustee account or the title company's trustee account. If you are buying directly from the owner, insist that your deposit be placed with the title company or at least a neutral third party.

2. *LOAN TRUST FUNDS*
    When assuming an FHA or GI loan, always take the seller's loan trust funds (impounds which the lender collects to pay tax and insurance bills on the property). By taking over the trust funds your total closing costs in an assumption purchase should be less than $400 as opposed to closing costs of well over $1,000 on a new conventional loan. A more detailed look at loan trust funds is contained in Chapter IX.

3. *TERMITE CLAUSE*
    Always have a termite inspection on the property you are buying and insist that the seller pay for all corrective work needed. It isn't just bugs you are looking for. Termite (structural pest control) reports call for correction of all dry-rot

conditions, among other things. The only exception I make to this rule is when there is a recent report not more than five months old.

4. *WARRANTIES*
   If the deposit receipt or purchase contract you are using does not call for some type of property warranty, the following clause is a must. Write into your contract "seller warrants that grounds and improvements will be maintained, that roof is water-tight, and that all appliances and heating, plumbing, sewer, and electrical systems shall be in working order at close of escrow. Seller agrees to permit inspection thereof prior to close of escrow and to pay for any necessary repairs." That clause is part of the Contra Costa Board of Realtors standard purchase agreement.

5. *PERSONAL PROPERTY*
   You will have a hard time renting a home that does not have a stove and window coverings. If they are in good repair be sure and ask for them in your sales contract.

Psychology of the Sale

Hundreds of books have been written on the psychology of buying and selling. I am not going to attempt a detailed discussion of the subject, but herein are a few important considerations to keep in mind when involved in negotiations.

It is very difficult to confront a seller, face to face, and tell him that you are offering $1,000 less than his asking price because his home is dirty as well as overpriced. This is one important reason why your Realtor has an advantage over you, the principal. The Realtor can act as a neutral party because he is not emotionally involved. And with his training and experience, your Realtor can most likely strike a better bargain than you can.

But if you find yourself in negotiations directly with an owner, remember he may be playing the game of "counter-offer." No matter how good your offer is, the seller may insist upon a counter-offer. If this is the case, be prepared. First of all, try to find out the recent selling prices of comparable homes in the neighborhood. Explain to the seller, without becoming emotionally involved, that your offer is fair and is based upon recent neighborhood sales. Be prepared to compromise a little — your original offer should be as much as $500 below what you will really pay for the property. If you are unable to get your original offer accepted, you can then offer to compromise by coming up $500 in price.

In most cases you should be successful after your first round of negotiations. If not — retreat. Tell the seller that you must have a decision today and that you will return in one hour so he can have time to think.

As I have pointed out, it is ridiculous to haggle over a few hundred dollars in light of how much homes appreciate in value each year. Prior to returning to the seller's home you must decide how badly you want the property. Ask yourself if it is really a good loan and is it really a clean and well cared for home. If the answer is yes, then you might want to raise the ante another few hundred dollars if the seller greets you with a "no." If you decide the home is not really worth it, then be prepared to say "Thank you, but no."

Loan Discount Points

Loan discount points are a necessary evil that must be paid by a seller if a buyer is to obtain a new FHA or GI loan. Each point is 1 per cent of the buyer's new loan. So 1 point on a $30,000 loan would be $300. Over the past five years I have seen the points charged range from 0 to 8.

The U.S. Government will not allow the buyer to pay these points. At the same time the government sets the FHA and GI interest rates at a percentage almost always beneath conventional loan rates. And because the money for FHA & GI loans is private (Uncle Sam only insures the lender against default) the lender requires a bonus (points) so that his return will be the same for all loans he makes.

This discussion is important for investment purposes for only one reason. Many times you will find a good assumption buy which is disguised because the price may include six points. On a $30,000 home six points represents $1,800. This same home could have a good assumable loan of $24,000. But for practical purposes the amount of cash you would need in order to buy is $4,200 — not $6,000.

The reason is quite simple. When a seller agrees to pay points he in effect agrees to lose that amount of money. Thus, 95 per cent of the time you will be able to discount these points. In this particular example, you should offer $3,500 cash to loan (or $27,500 sale price).

I suggest offering $700 less than what you discount for the six points for two reasons. First of all, your offer should be somewhat less than what you are really willing to pay. Secondly, when a seller is willing to sell FHA and GI, he is gambling that his home will appraise for the asking price. But government appraisals are sometimes erratic and low. And it often takes a month to get the results. An assumption sale is greatly preferred over an FHA or GI sale. A wise seller would take a few hundred dollars less for a firm sale rather than gamble.

Be alert! As loan discount points rise, your chances of a good buy increase; a good buy that will be considerably beneath market value.

Searching for Rental Property

Recently I met a lady who began looking for a rental home immediately after reading the first edition of *The Monopoly Game*. One whole year had passed and she didn't find one. In that one year home values increased by over $10,000.

I recommend the virtue of patience when looking for property. You may have to inspect dozens of homes over a two- or three-month period before you find the right one. But take aim at what you want and act fast when you make the decision to buy a property. Time is money.

Here are some ideas that may help you. Before starting your property search, decide on what basic *location* you want, determine the *condition* you want the home to be in (in other words, are you willing to paint and re-carpet?) and arrange your financing (will you be looking for an assumption or conventional terms?).

If real estate sales are slow you will probably find yourself in a buyers market. This is the very best time to buy property at prices lower than market value. If sales are brisk you are probably looking in a sellers market. This is the most difficult situation for the investor as you will probably have competition on every good home you might want to buy. In a sellers market you will have to work extra hard in finding the type of property you want.

Start your search with the assistance of a good Realtor. Make sure he or she is competent and loyal. Your Realtor must understand investments, have the time available to work with you, and agree not to compete with you for the good buys. If your Realtor can do all this and if you are comfortable with him—then go to work. If not, look around for another. But the important thing to remember is to work with only one agent at a time. If you work with more than one you will not get good service.

Don't neglect "For Sale by Owner" ads in your local newspaper. But don't get in over your head. While you might stumble onto an easy assumption, do not attempt more complicated sales without the help of your Realtor. It is always wise to use a neutral third party in negotiations between principals in a transaction. This can save you thousands of dollars in the long run.

In searching for property, don't leave any stones unturned. Insist that your Realtor thoroughly check all new multiple listings as they come out. At the same time you can drive by the neighborhoods that you like best and look for new "For Sale" signs. In some Realty boards, all new listings must be immediately placed on the Multiple Listing Service. But in others it is the option of the seller and agent so therefore some of the best homes are not placed on the service. Thus you have to work harder to find these good listings.

Buying Tips

A lot of good rental property buys are passed up because the would-be purchaser cannot visualize himself living in the home. That is a big mistake. You are not going to live in the home—your tenant is. You must learn to throw all personal preferences out of your mind and review each prospective property on an objective basis. It doesn't matter if the home has only 1,000 square feet and one bathroom if it does two things: Rents easily and will appreciate in value.

Here are some tips on what *is* important and what *is not* important for your rental property.

Age: Age is not really an important issue. If you have a choice between a home which is 5 years old and a home 25 years old, take the younger property provided all other considerations are about equal. While it is often true that many older homes are constructed a lot better than many of the newer properties, the newer home will usually have more attractive extras to enhance its value.

Size: The size of a home is often relative to the price—as long as you are comparing properties in a similar neighborhood. The size of a home will not alter your leverage and appreciation percentages. In other words, a two-bedroom home will appreciate as rapidly as a four-bedroom home. Your decision to buy or not to buy a smaller home will probably be based upon either current opportunity or your available cash as a smaller home would normally require less capital outlay.

I prefer owning three- or four-bedroom properties. However, I have had excellent results with two-bedroom homes and would not hesitate to buy another. The only real advantage of a three-bedroom home is that it has a wider resale market.

Price: As a general guideline, purchase property that falls in the lower to middle price range of your community. Eliminate the extremes.

Let's assume that your area has an average home price of $40,000 with the lows beginning at $20,000 and the high reaching to $90,000. You will find that the best price range for rental property will be between $25,000 and $50,000. The lowest priced homes ($20,000) will probably be too small, old, rundown or may attract tenants who will cause the most problems. The higher priced homes will be more difficult to find tenants for unless your community has a very high number of short-term corporate transfers.

Amenities: Amenities are the plusses in favor of a property because of location or improvement factors.

It goes without saying that the more amenities a rental property has the better it is for you. But you can't always get all the amenities you want in your price range and that's okay, too.

A good example would be central air conditioning in the warmer areas of the Southwest. Air conditioning is an amenity that most homes have, especially those that are newer and more expensive. Suppose that you live in a Southwestern community where the average home sells for $40,000 and that nearly all homes above that figure have central air and most of those below the average do not. Given these facts it is necessary to have central air in a rental valued at about $40,000 or more. And by the same token it is not necessary for a home below $40,000.

The same thing can be said for basements in the Midwest. If 90 per cent of the homes in your community have basements then I would not recommend a rental property without one.

Other desirable amenities would include garbage disposal, double car garage, built-in range and oven, and wall to wall carpeting. They are all nice to have but only necessary if they are demanded by the majority in your community or if they are expected in the price range of the home you are buying. Never hesitate to buy a home without extras as long as it is consistent with the price range you are buying in.

On the following page is a checklist
that can help you
pick out the right home:

A Checklist to help you find
The Right Home

The Neighborhood:

- ☐ Is the neighborhood well cared for?
- ☐ Are other homes in the same price range?
- ☐ Are all municipal services available?
- ☐ Is there good access to public transportation?
- ☐ Is there adequate shopping nearby?
- ☐ Is there adequate parking?
- ☐ Is the quality of schools good?
- ☐ Are there any hazardous traffic patterns?
- ☐ Are there any special noise problems?
- ☐ Are the property taxes in line with other areas?
- ☐ Are property values raising?

The Yard:

- ☐ Is the size of the yard adequate?
- ☐ Is the general condition of the yard good?
- ☐ Does any landscaping need replacement?
- ☐ Are there any dead trees?
- ☐ Are all fences, retaining walls and walkways in good repair?
- ☐ Is the drainage away from the foundation?
- ☐ If the home has a septic tank, has it been recently serviced?

The Home:

- ☐ Are the range and oven included in the price?
- ☐ Is the furnace working properly?
- ☐ Does the water heater have good life left?
- ☐ Is there a 220 volt line for range and dryer?
- ☐ Is the electrical service adequate?
- ☐ Is the condition of the exterior paint adequate?
- ☐ Is the condition of the interior paint adequate?
- ☐ Is the roof water-tight? Will it be in the near future?
- ☐ Are all floors and floor coverings in good repair?
- ☐ Is the condition of the windows and window sashes adequate?
- ☐ Is the building structurally sound?
- ☐ If there are any additions or alterations, were the necessary permits filed?
- ☐ Are walls and ceilings free from any minor cracks?
- ☐ Is there ample wall space for furniture?
- ☐ Is there adequate closet and storage space?
- ☐ Do all windows have coverings or draperies and are they in acceptable condition?
- ☐ Are kitchen countertops and cabinets in good repair?
- ☐ Is the basement free of any water marks, wet cracks, signs of moisture?
- ☐ Is there any problem which will require an immediate outlay of cash?
- ☐ Is the garage wide and long enough for adequate parking?

V

Maintaining and Renting
Your Property

A tale of two landlords: The first one was a kind man but he was too demanding; the second one was a little lazy and did not pay enough attention to his investments. They are both out of the rental business now.

The first landlord wanted his rental home to look just like his personal home — neat and clean and completely weed-free. When his tenants did not mow the lawn just right he would do it for them. Needless to say he got tired of that fast and sold his rental.

The second landlord failed to call the tenants when the rent was overdue and he never bothered to check up on the condition of his property. One day, after his vacant and run-down home had gone 45 days without any interest from prospective tenants, he decided to sell. He didn't see the profit that could be made . . . only the trouble.

What may sound difficult really isn't. It's the fourth success factor . . . *Maintenance* of your property. As you will see, many unguided investors buy their first property and then "blow it" with poor management. There is nothing difficult or mysterious about renting and taking care of your property (even if you have 10 or 12 homes). Just follow a few simple guidelines and you WILL be successful.

Start With The Property

To have a successful investment portfolio you must obtain the best tenants available in your area. To get the best tenants you must have the best homes. And when you get the best tenants your property will be kept in better condition and thus save you a lot of dollars in the long run.

To obtain top quality tenants you *must* not show your property until the home is ready. If you have just bought a clean, ready-to-go property, then you can rent it at close of escrow. But if the lawn needs cutting—cut it; if it badly needs a new paint job—paint it; if the oven needs cleaning—clean it; or if new carpeting is needed—install it. Remember that to attract a better than average tenant your property must be in better than average condition.

Advertising

There are several inexpensive but limited methods of advertising for new tenants. They would include lawn and window signs; notices on grocery store and company bulletin boards; and placement of lease listings through your Realtor on the local multiple listing service.

But none of these methods come even close to being as effective as newspaper advertising. That is where the action is! The cost can be high, largely depending upon the circulation and rates of your local newspaper. But consider this one important fact. Isn't it better to spend $50 to $75 in newspaper advertising than to lose $300 in rent because the property went vacant for a month?

If you have more than one newspaper in your community, always start with the one that has the largest classified news section. Maybe it is more expensive, but if it's where the classified action is then it's where you want to be. Free newspapers and throw-aways, incidentally, will usually get you very few ad calls. So don't put too much hope in them.

Don't spare the buck if you want to get your home rented fast. Do not advertise only on Sundays. I have found that people would rather do just about anything else on Sundays than look at real estate. When I run an ad which begins Sunday and runs into the weekdays I will get twice as many calls on Monday or Tuesday than I will on Sunday. If necessary, put your home telephone number in the ad for Sunday and evening calls, and your work number (if allowed) in the ad for weekdays.

When writing your ad—be creative and don't mince words. And watch out for abbreviations that readers may not understand. Here are samples of two contrasting ads:

THE WRONG WAY:

Clean 3 bdrm., 2 bath, house on big lot with trees. Fm. room, AEK, cpts and full basement. $350 mo., lease, references required. Call 689-5090.

A BETTER WAY:

PLEASANT HILL—Charming and secluded 3 bedroom, 2 bath, ranch style home on big 1/3 acre lot protected by tall pine and oak trees. Immaculate condition! Full basement with wet bar, upstairs family room and roomy kitchen with built-in electric appliances. Wall-to-wall carpeting throughout. Lease for only $350. Call 689-5090.

The second ad is going to cost you twice as much money to run. But don't you think it will get maybe four or five times more ad calls? Note the second ad begins with the city. Always identify the price as well as the city or section of town. Don't spare the adjectives. Feature with lavish praise the best qualities of your home.

Don't let your ads become stale. Prospective tenants are looking in the paper every day. If after one week you do not rent your home then write a new ad and from a fresh angle.

By the way, you are probably going to get many more phone calls from a good ad than you can handle. So pre-qualify over the telephone. Don't make an appointment with everyone. Select only those whom you want and those that earn enough money to afford your home.

Selecting Your Tenant

Select the proper tenant for your property! It is not really difficult if you have a tenant checklist and stick to it.

After placing a "For Lease" sign on the lawn and a "For Lease" ad in your local newspaper, be prepared to stand eyeball to eyeball with your prospective tenant. Be prepared—with the aid of a checklist of your tenant qualifications. The only hard thing here is to learn to say no. For many people saying the word "no" comes hard and this is where you can get into trouble. If your checklist for a certain property calls for the tenant to have a gross income of $1,000 per month and he only makes $800—then say no.

Your checklist need not be any more than a written list of the requirements you demand your tenants to meet. Because of non-discrimination laws it is important that you have such a list. You cannot turn down a tenant because of his race. But if a tenant does not meet your checklist requirements then you can turn him down, provided your requirements are fair, reasonable and apply to everyone. But be sure they are in writing.

A good example is in New York, where a state judge ruled that a landlord can refuse to rent to people because he dislikes their looks or jobs or even if they seem to be "intelligent persons, aware of their rights, who might give him trouble in the future." The only restriction: the landlord may not use race, creed, color, national origin, sex or marital status as criteria.

A few of the items which you might include on your checklist are as follows:

1. Minimum 3½ to 1 gross salary-to-rent ratio
2. Steady employment—one year or more
3. Clean credit report
4. References from last two landlords
5. Own a clean, well cared for automobile
6. No large "indoor" pet
7. No singles or roommates
8. No more than six persons for a three-bedroom home
9. Able to pay first and last month rent plus deposit
10. Banking references

Let's take a closer look at the checklist.

1. *Salary to rent ratio*

   If a prospective tenant earns only $800 per month, and you are asking $300 rent, then he obviously cannot afford the home. Lenders insist that home buyers earn at least 3½ times more gross income than what their mortgage payments will be. Some lenders even require a 4 to 1 ratio.

2. *Steady employment*

   It is good practice to only consider tenants that have been steadily employed for a year or more. There are major exceptions to this rule, however. Some exceptions would be: professionals beginning work after college or the service; school teachers; transferred executives or experienced salesmen or journeymen who have just changed jobs. The exceptions are many but this rule will keep you out of trouble with transients who have just moved to your community and have taken a new job—which may not last. It is also a good practice to make a telephone call to verify your prospective tenant's job and income.

3. *Credit report*

   Perhaps the best way to protect yourself against a bad tenant is to order a credit check from a reputable credit bureau. If the prospective tenant is a "bad apple," you will find out in time. Just the idea of a credit check will scare some away.

Most credit bureaus, however, will not accept an application placed by an individual. If you own several rentals it will probably pay off to join a credit bureau. If you are not that big yet ask your Realtor to arrange a credit report for you.

4. *Landlord references*

Be a skeptic! Place a telephone call to the prospective tenant's current and previous landlords, if possible. Be careful of the information you get from the tenant's current landlord—he may say anything to get rid of him. That is why it is a good insurance policy to check with a former landlord who can be completely honest.

Not many, but a few applicants will lie. I have caught several. Remember—in your community at this time some unfortunate landlord is in court evicting a bad tenant. After he is evicted, that tenant must find another place to live. He may reply to your ad, so be prepared.

5. *Clean automobile*

Find an excuse to take a look at your applicant's automobile. If the vehicle is clean and well kept, you can probably assume that your home will be cared for the same way. If the auto is a complete mess, you can imagine what they may do to your home. It would also be good to visit the applicant's present home if it can be arranged.

6. *Pets*

I like pets! I own a big German Shepherd that takes delight in tearing up my lawns and shrubberies. None of my tenants own a German Shepherd, however. I won't let them. I will allow a cat or a small house dog. If the tenants have a larger "outdoor" dog, insist the dog stay out of the home. To help insure against problems, increase their security deposit.

I know of one unlucky landlord who once rented a house to a couple with a huge St. Bernard. The house had new carpeting installed and a fine coat of paint to greet the new tenants. A year later the people and their St. Bernard moved out. But an obnoxious, musty dog odor stayed behind. The home remained vacant for over a month as the panicked owner tried everything to get rid of the odor. He twice shampooed the carpeting, repainted the walls, laundered the draperies and scrubbed the kitchen floors and appliances. He never did get completely rid of the odor. I can't tell you how this type of a dog odor is created—but I can warn you against too many pets or large pets.

7. *Singles and roommmates*

   You will have much better luck with a family or couple (even unmarried) than you will ever have with singles or roommates. I am defining singles and roommates as two or more people living together as a temporary convenience. They may be a group of four college girls or three young men working at jobs that are not too steady. The odds are great that you will have trouble.

   Roommates I will accept must be over 25 years of age and must have a good and steady occupation.

   If you are compelled to accept roommates you should do two things. First of all, have each of them sign the lease agreement and have a written understanding that they are to make no substitutions. In other words, if one moves out, any replacement must be approved by you and he or she must sign the lease agreement. Without your acceptance of a replacement, all parties to the lease will remain liable for rent, etc.

   Secondly, if your roommates are under the age of 25, insist that their parents (or a legal guardian) sign a statement making them also liable for rent payments and damages. I am aware that a person is now a legal adult at age 18. But the choice is yours. If your checklist says no singles or roommates under age 25, then they don't rent your property unless they play the game according to your rules.

   A third method of accepting roommates is to designate one of the tenants to sign the lease and take full responsibility for his partners. This person should be able to qualify on your gross salary-to-rent ratio on his or her own merit. By using this method you should be able to avoid any trouble with the new anti-age discrimination laws that are popping up throughout our land. At this writing, however, there are no federal laws prohibiting discrimination because of age.

8. *People limit*

   Limit the number of persons who may occupy your property. It would be ridiculous (and destructive) to have a family of eight living in a two-bedroom home. Make your own rules, but I suggest no more than four for a two-bedroom; six for a three-bedroom; eight for a four-bedroom; and 10 for a five-bedroom. These figures are more than fair.

9. *First and last month's rent*

   It is always wise to collect first and last month's rent plus either a damage or cleaning deposit *before* your tenant is given possession. I believe that if a person does not have this money before occupancy, this is an indication he may have trouble paying rent down the road. I am highly suspicious of a family with only $200 or $300 cash to their name.

Again there may be exeptions worth considering. My very first tenant (and one of the best I've ever had) could not pay his last month's rent in advance. I let him pay it in four equal monthly installments. The reason—he and his wife, both just recently employed, were just a month or so out of college and had just moved to California to begin their respective careers.

10. *Banking references*
I have found that if a person does not have a bank checking account—there may be a reason. One reason could be that the bank would not allow him to have a checking account because of previous bad check problems. While this is not always the reason, you should take a close look at any applicants who do not have a checking account.

When your applicant does give you a check, be sure to telephone the bank to verify that enough funds are on deposit to cover the check.

Where Will The Tenants Come From?

Why do people rent rather than buy? Will there always be enough tenants to occupy all the rental units available now and in the future? These are not frivolous questions. I am asked them all the time.

The availability of tenants often runs in cycles. There are usually more tenants available after a run of high interest rates. And that is understandable because many first-home buyers as well as investors will wait until interest rates drop. When rates jump from 8½ per cent to 9½ per cent, the monthly cost per $1,000 of a 30-year mortgage increases by 72 cents. For a $30,000 loan that is a $21.60 monthly increase.

There are three reasons that will help to supply an abundant number of tenants over the next several years. The first is the natural population increases. As pointed out in Chapter III, our nation's population is still increasing at almost alarming rates.

The second reason has to do with the post-Korean War baby boom. During the next 10 years the total number of households will increase by 22 per cent. Thus demand for new housing will be higher than ever in the next 10 years. But at today's production levels we are falling far short of meeting that demand. This problem is made even bigger when you consider that new multi-family starts are significantly below previous levels. This is partially because apartment builders are concerned with problems such as soaring operating costs, rent controls, unreasonable zoning policies and urban tenants who are demanding more than landlords can provide.

A third reason has more meaning in the West than in other parts of the country. As I pointed out in Chapter III, I do not believe that American families are being priced out of the home market. But there is a temporary exception to that premise. Partially because of migration trends to the South and West, many Western states experienced almost two years of runaway inflation. In some California communities homes appreciated more than 50 per cent during that period.

The results of this phenomenon are two-fold. First of all, a short-term slowing period in rising real estate values is likely to occur. Secondly, many persons are priced out of the market in this kind of a situation. This means that a greater number of renters will be available during the next few years in the communities that had this rapid appreciation.

All signs point to more than enough tenants to keep the investor's properties filled up for a long, long time.

Tenants Come In Seven Types

From experience, I have found that tenants can be placed in seven different categories, with some overlapping. By understanding why people rent you will be better able to deal with them. They are:

1. Corporate Transfers
2. Potential Home Buyers
3. Young Families
4. Old Families (Retired)
5. Adult Singles
6. Young Singles and Roommates
7. Perennial Renters

I mention these seven types of tenants not to warn you against a certain category but to recommend different approaches to use.

1. *Corporate Transfers*
   In some areas of our country, literally thousands of families are on the move every year. Often their company pays moving

expenses. I have found that the vast majority of corporate families make excellent tenants. But you must be prepared to do one special thing for them — and that is to allow them to break their lease if and when their company says go.

2. *Potential Home Buyers*
This category contains those people who are either between homes or are marking time before they buy their own residence. I find that most families in this category are excellent tenants. And needless to say, they can be a bonanza for the Realtor-landlord who is eyeing a future sales commission. The non-Realtor must be careful! Either go with a month-to-month rental agreement or write a penalty agreement into your lease contract in the event the full term is not reached. The penalty could call for loss of security deposit and/or all advertising costs and lost rents due to their early departure.

3. *Young Families*
This type of tenant is probably two or three years away from buying their own home. They can make excellent tenants but sometimes their job situation is not very secure. Tenants in this category are more likely than any of the others to improve your home so as to actually increase its value.

4. *Old Families (Retirees)*
Most people in this class have owned their own home at one time and now find themselves without children and without the need to have a large home. They are about to retire or already have. Many excellent tenants come from this group.

5. *Adult Singles*
Perhaps recently divorced or widowed, this group can range from excellent to poor as far as tenant ratings go. Many divorced women receive support payments which can suddenly stop — before a good-paying or stable job can be found. A person may pass your checklist requirements now, but how about the future? You might want to put any suspects on a month-to-month rental basis rather than a lease.

6. *Young Singles and Roommates*
I hate to say it — but in this category you have approximately 50-50 odds that you will have trouble. Special care is needed when renting or leasing to people in this category. See item 7 of the preceding checklist.

7. *Perennial Renters*
These are the people that always have and always will rent. Many cannot qualify for a real estate loan and many simply do not believe in the benefits of property ownership. By the same

token some of them have little respect for their landlord. Millions of Americans are in this category—so you cannot avoid them. Without the perennial tenant, rental property investments would not be as lucrative as they are. It is primarily for this type of tenant that you need to carefully follow your checklist.

A good example comes to mind from a note I recently received from a sorry but wiser competitor. It warned of a couple in their early 60's who appear as sweet and innocent as possible. Except Mr. & Mrs. Sweetness did not pay any rent for eight months. In fact Mr. Sweetness' deposit check was written on a bank account closed two years prior. The evicting sheriff was quite familiar with the lovely couple. He said they simply move from place to place, pay no rent, and wait for eviction. The sheriff said the couple has been doing this for about 25 years. If my competitor used a checklist (and credit report) he NEVER would have been stuck.

Put It In Writing

Make sure all agreements between yourself and your tenants are in writing. Verbal agreements do not carry any weight in court. Use a lease or rental contract that calls for a $10.00 or more late payment charge if the rent is over five days delinquent. This one small item will save headaches later on. Few tenants will allow themselves to get into a position to pay a late charge. After being socked with a $10 charge, they won't be too busy to write their rent check next time around.

• On the following pages is a facsimile of the Lease Rental Agreement form which I prefer to use, presented here through the courtesy of its publisher so that you can look over the points covered:—

LEASE-RENTAL AGREEMENT AND DEPOSIT RECEIPT

RECEIVED FROM ....

.... hereinafter referred to as Tenant.

the sum of $ .... (.... DOLLARS),

evidenced by ...., as a deposit which, upon acceptance of this rental agreement, shall belong to
the Owner of the premises, hereinafter referred to as Owner and shall be applied as follows:

	RECEIVED	PAYABLE PRIOR TO OCCUPANCY
Rent for the period from .... to	$	$ ....
Last .... month's rent	$	$ ....
Security deposit	$	$ ....
Key Deposit	$	$ ....
Cleaning charge	$	$ ....
Other	$	$ ....
TOTAL	$	$ ....

In the event that this agreement is not accepted by the Owner or his authorized agent, within .... days, the total deposit received shall be refunded.

Tenant hereby offers to rent from the Owner the premises situated in the City of ...., County of ....,

State of ...., described as ...., consisting of ....,
upon the following TERMS and CONDITIONS:

TERM: The term hereof shall commence on ...., 19 ....,

☐ until ...., 19 ....

☐ on a month-to-month basis thereafter, until either party shall terminate the same by giving the other party .... days written notice delivered by certified mail, provided that Tenant agrees not to terminate prior to the expiration of .... months.

RENT: Rent shall be $ .... per month, payable in advance, upon the .... day of each calendar month to Owner or his authorized agent, at the following address: .... 19 ...., and continue (check one of the two following alternatives): or at such other places as may be designated by Owner from time to time. In the event rent is not paid within five (5) days after due date, Tenant agrees to pay a late charge of $10.00. Tenant agrees further to pay $5.00 for each dishonored bank check.

MULTIPLE OCCUPANCY: It is expressly understood that this agreement is between the Owner and each signatory individually and severally. In the event of default by any one signatory each and every remaining signatory shall be responsible for timely payment of rent and all other provisions of this agreement.

UTILITIES: Tenant shall be responsible for the payment of all utilities and services, except: _____ which shall be paid by Owner.

USE: The premises shall be used as a residence with no more than _____ adults and _____ children, and for no other purpose, without the prior written consent of the Owner. Occupancy by guests staying over 15 days will be considered to be in violation of this provision.

PETS: No pets shall be brought on the premises without the prior written consent of the Owner.

HOUSE RULES: In the event that the premises are a portion of a building containing more than one unit, Tenant agrees to abide by any and all house rules, whether promulgated before or after the execution hereof, including, but not limited to, rules with respect to noise, odors, disposal of refuse, pets, parking, and use of common areas. Tenant shall not have a waterbed on the premises without prior written consent of the Owner.

ORDINANCES AND STATUTES: Tenant shall comply with all statutes, ordinances and requirements of all municipal, state and federal authorities now in force, or which may hereafter be in force, pertaining to the use of the premises.

ASSIGNMENT AND SUBLETTING: Tenant shall not assign this agreement or sublet any portion of the premises without prior written consent of the Owner which may not be unreasonably withheld.

MAINTENANCE, REPAIRS OR ALTERATIONS: Tenant acknowledges that the premises are in good order and repair, unless otherwise indicated herein. Owner may at any time give Tenant a written inventory of furniture and furnishings on the premises and Tenant shall be deemed to have possession of all said furniture and furnishings in good condition and repair, unless he objects thereto in writing within five days after receipt of such inventory. Tenant shall, at his own expense, and at all times, maintain the premises in a clean and sanitary manner including all equipment, appliances, furniture and furnishings therein and shall surrender the same, at termination hereof, in as good condition as received, normal wear and tear excepted. Tenant shall be responsible for all repairs required for exposed plumbing or electrical wiring and for damages caused by his negligence and that of his family or invitees or guests. Tenant shall not paint, paper or otherwise redecorate or make alterations to the premises without the prior written consent of the Owner. Tenant shall irrigate and maintain any surrounding grounds, including lawns and shrubbery, and keep the same clear of rubbish or weeds if such grounds are a part of the premises and are exclusively for the use of the Tenant.

ENTRY AND INSPECTION: Tenant shall permit Owner or Owner's agents to enter the premises at reasonable times and upon reasonable notice for the purpose of inspecting the premises or showing the same to prospective tenants or purchasers, or for making necessary repairs.

INDEMNIFICATION: Owner shall not be liable for any damage or injury to Tenant, or any other person, or to any property, occurring on the premises, or any part thereof, or in common areas thereof, and Tenant agrees to hold Owner harmless from any claims for damages no matter how caused.

POSSESSION: If Owner is unable to deliver possession of the premises at the commencement hereof, Owner shall not be liable for any damage caused thereby, nor shall this agreement be void or voidable, but Tenant shall not be liable for any rent until possession is delivered. Tenant may terminate this agreement if possession is not delivered within _____ days of the commencement of the term hereof.

DEFAULT: Any failure by Tenant to pay rent when due, or perform any term hereof, shall, at the option of the Owner, terminate all rights of Tenant hereunder. In the event that Tenant shall be absent from the premises for a period of 5 consecutive days, while in default, Tenant shall, at the option of the Owner, be deemed to have abandoned the premises and any property left on the premises shall be considered abandoned and may be disposed of by Owner as he shall see fit. All property on the premises is hereby subject to a lien in favor of Owner, for payment of all sums due hereunder, to the maximum extent allowed by law.

In the event of a default by Tenant, Owner may elect to (a) continue the lease in effect and enforce all his rights and remedies hereunder, including the right to recover the rent as it becomes due, or (b) at any time, terminate all of Tenant's rights hereunder and recover from Tenant all damages he may incur by reason of the breach of the lease, including the cost of recovering the premises, and including the worth at the time of such termination, or at the time of an award if suit be instituted to enforce this provision, of the amount by which the unpaid rent for the balance of the term exceeds the amount of such rental loss which the tenant proves could be reasonably avoided.

SECURITY: The security deposit set forth above, if any, shall secure the performance of Tenant's obligations hereunder. Owner may, but shall not be obligated to, apply all or portions of said deposit on account of Tenant's obligations hereunder. Any balance remaining upon termination shall be returned to Tenant. Tenant shall not have the right to apply the Security Deposit in payment of the last month's rent.

DEPOSIT REFUNDS: Any returnable deposits shall be refunded within two weeks from date possession is delivered to Owner or his Authorized Agent.

ATTORNEYS FEES: In the event that Owner shall prevail in any legal action brought by either party to enforce the terms hereof or relating to the demised premises, Owner shall be entitled to all costs incurred in connection with such action, including a reasonable attorney's fee.

WAIVER: No failure of Owner to enforce any term hereof shall be deemed a waiver, nor shall any acceptance of a partial payment of rent be deemed a waiver of Owner's right to the full amount thereof.

NOTICES: Any notice which either party may or is required to give, may be given by mailing the same, postage prepaid, to Tenant at the premises or to Owner at the address shown below or at such other places as may be designated by the parties from time to time.

HOLDING OVER: Any holding over after expiration hereof, with the consent of Owner, shall be construed as a month-to-month tenancy in accordance with the terms hereof, as applicable.

TIME: Time is of the essence of this agreement.

ADDITIONAL TERMS AND CONDITIONS:

ENTIRE AGREEMENT: The foregoing constitutes the entire agreement between the parties and may be modified only by a writing signed by both parties. The following Exhibits, if any, have been made a part of this agreement before the parties' execution hereof: ....

The undersigned Tenant hereby acknowledges receipt of a copy hereof.   DATED.........................

....Agent   ....Tenant

....Address/Phone   ....Tenant

By...   ....Address/Phone

FORM 105 (6-3-74)   © COPYRIGHT, 1970, BY PROFESSIONAL PUBLISHING CORP., 122 PAUL DRIVE, SAN RAFAEL, CALIFORNIA 94903

CONTINUED ON REVERSE SIDE

ACCEPTANCE

The undersigned Owner accepts the foregoing offer and agrees to rent the herein described premises on the terms and conditions herein specified. The Owner agrees to pay to................., the Agent in this transaction, the sum of $................ (..............................DOLLARS) for services rendered and authorizes Agent to deduct said sum from the deposit received from Lessee. This agreement shall not limit the rights of Agent provided for in any listing or other agreement which may be in effect between Lessor and Agent.

The undersigned Owner hereby acknowledges receipt of a copy hereof.

DATED:................

................Owner's Authorized Agent

................Owner

................Address

................Phone

By................

TENANT'S PERSONAL AND CREDIT INFORMATION

PERSONAL DATA

Anticipated length of occupancy

	Date of Birth	Social Security No.	
Name		Drivers Lic. No.	Expir. Date
		Social Security No.	
Name of Spouse		Drivers Lic. No.	Expir. Date
Present Address	Res. Phone	Bus. Phone	

How long at present address _____ Landlord or Agent _____ Phone _____

How long at previous address _____ Landlord or Agent _____ Phone _____

Legal Status: Single _____ Married _____ Divorced _____ Widowed _____

Occupants: Relationships: _____ Ages: _____ Pets? _____

Car Make _____ Year _____ Model _____ Color _____ License No. _____

OCCUPATION

	PRESENT OCCUPATION *	PRIOR OCCUPATION *	SPOUSE'S OCCUPATION
Occupation			
Employer			
Self-employed, d.b.a.			
Business Address			
Business Phone			
Type of Business			
Position held			
Name and Title of Superior			
How long			
Monthly Gross Income			

*If employed or self-employed less than two years, give same information on prior occupation.

REFERENCES

Bank Reference .... Address .... Phone ....

CREDIT REFERENCE	ADDRESS	HIGHEST AMOUNT OWED	PURPOSE OF CREDIT	ACCOUNT OPEN OR DATE CLOSED

PERSONAL REFERENCE	ADDRESS	PHONE	LENGTH OF ACQUAINTANCE	OCCUPATION

NEAREST RELATIVE	ADDRESS	PHONE	CITY	RELATIONSHIP

Have you ever filed a petition in bankruptcy?............Have you ever been evicted from any tenancy?............
Have you ever wilfully and intentionally refused to pay any rent when due?............

I DECLARE THE FOREGOING TO BE TRUE UNDER PENALTY OF PERJURY.
I agree that Landlord may terminate any agreement entered into in reliance on any misstatement made above.

DATED:............

............Applicant

............Applicant

If you would like a supply of this form, which I use both personally and professionally, write to Professional Publishing Corporation, Box 4187, San Rafael, California 94903. Their Form 105, Lease Rental Agreement and Deposit Receipt is excellent and easy to use. At this writing a pad of 50 forms costs $2.65 plus a $1.00 shipping and handling charge.

Lease Or Rental Agreement?

Most professionals cannot agree among themselves on whether or not it is better to lease or to rent. I prefer the lease—especially for a term of one year.

With the lease agreement you cannot evict the tenants (unless with proper cause) or raise the rent until the contract expires. This gives security to both you and your tenant. With a month-to-month rental agreement your tenant can leave by giving 30 days notice. There is nothing more exasperating than having a tenant give you 30 days notice after just living in the property for two months.

Some landlords do not want a year's lease because they cannot raise the rent. I say that a good manager will be able to know one year in advance what rent he needs and can get from the property. There is no need to raise rents every few months.

If you have an opportunity to take a two-year lease—don't do it. Write a one-year lease instead with the tenants having an option for the second year at a higher rent payment. This also gives you an opportunity to cancel out after one year if the tenant does not properly maintain your home.

Breaking The Lease

Sometimes things don't go along as planned. Often a tenant wants to move before the lease runs out. This need not be a major problem. If and when it happens to you—don't run down to your attorney. Let the tenant break the lease provided that he will pay for any lost revenue you may suffer. This is one good reason why you should always collect a last month's rent or a security deposit.

By moving out before expiration of the lease, the tenant does not get off the hook. He is legally bound to pay rent for the full lease term whether or not he continues occupancy. You can get a judgment to collect the monies owed. But in California, the law says that the landlord must take all steps necessary to keep his damages to a minimum. So you must begin looking for a new tenant, with or without your tenant's cooperation.

After receiving notice from your tenant, ask for his cooperation. Immediately begin looking for a new tenant. Tell your tenant that he can break the lease provided that he will pay for any rent or commission losses you may suffer. After all, if it goes to court, this is all the money you will probably get anyway.

It isn't so easy when the landlord wants to break the lease—even for just cause. The first thing to do is to give your tenant 30 days notice with an explanation of why you want him to move. You might even consider allowing one month free rent. If your notice and explanation do not do the job—you have a problem, even though the tenant may have broken the lease. Your next step would be eviction.

Eviction

Eviction is the common term for the process of forcing a tenant out of your property by legally going to court using an action called "unlawful detainer." I do not recommend the eviction process, except as a very last resort, as it is expensive and time consuming.

Avoid eviction by being a good landlord! I told you how to select the right tenant and how to be a fair landlord. The procedures set out are the best insurance against a bad tenant and thus an unlawful detainer action.

But if things don't work out—and you end up with a tenant who cannot pay rent or a tenant who is destroying your property— prepare to act. And don't delay! If your tenant is as much as 10 days late with his rent, call him and ask for payment plus late charge. If the payment does not arrive in another five days, pay him a personal visit armed with a "3-day notice to pay or quit."

Incidentally, if your tenant calls you in advance to advise you that his rent will be late, be lenient. If your tenant has a good history, give him the benefit of the doubt. I have waited as much as 20 days before and I have never been sorry. In fact, over the years I have had nearly 50 different tenants and only once have I had to ask a tenant to move and never have I had to file an unlawful detainer action.

In California the eviction process starts with the delivery of a "3-day notice to pay or quit." The notice, which can be purchased at most office supply stores, must describe the property in question and state the amount of rent due. It must also give the tenant the choice of paying or leaving. The notice can also be given for other lease breaches, like an unauthorized pet. To be effective the notice must specify the fault and demand correction within three days or the tenant must move out.

If your tenant problems are serious enough where you want him to leave the property, you can also deliver a 30-day notice to vacate. If your tenant is on a lease, rather than a month-to-month rental, be sure that he has actually violated the written lease agreement.

Incidentally, a 3-day notice must be served in person or (if no one is at home) it may be posted in a conspicuous place and a copy sent by certified mail. A 30-day notice may be served by first class mail. Also do not accept partial rent payment unless you are willing to start the 3-day notice procedure all over again.

Most tenants will either pay or leave after delivery of the 3-day notice. If they don't, however, you should immediately consult your attorney. And your attorney should be a specialist or at least competent in the area of evictions. He will complete the unlawful detainer action in the local Municipal Court or will advise you to follow through yourself in Small Claims Court if possible. However, in California you cannot use Small Claims Court to evict if your tenant is on a lease or if the rent or damages exceed $750.

Deposits

There are two types of deposits which you must be familiar with. The first is the earnest money deposit which you collect at the time the lease or rental contract is signed. The second type would be a cleaning charge or security deposit.

As most lease agreements are signed a week or two prior to occupancy, you must collect a substantial earnest money deposit which in effect holds the property until the balance of the money is paid and the keys are handed to the new tenants. I like to collect at least 50 per cent of the first month's rent. This deposit, upon acceptance of the agreement, becomes the property of the owner. If the tenant later changes his mind, he loses the deposit. After all, he has taken your house off the market.

A security deposit (which some landlords collect instead of last month rent) is to secure the tenant's lease obligations, including loss of rent or damage to the property.

A cleaning charge is not intended to be refundable. However, a recent California court decision holds that the charge is considered a deposit which the landlord must return if the tenant leaves the property in good condition.

Tenants should fully understand that they will get their cleaning charge back if the home is left in proper condition. This includes a clean range and oven, vacuumed carpeting, outdoor debris removed, etc. Expect normal wear and tear, but if walls are marred too badly use the cleaning charge for a new paint job.

Your cleaning charge should be somewhere between $50 and $100. And don't be a softie. If the tenant's job is not satisfactory, give them a little extra time. If they refuse, or if they still don't do the job right, withhold whatever amount is needed to hire a cleaning service to do the job.

The best course to follow is to collect a security deposit. I recommend either collecting first and last month's rent plus a $100 security deposit or collect a security deposit equal to the last month's rent (in lieu of the last month's rent).

The reason for this is that your security deposit can be used against loss of rent, damage to the property and to cover cleaning costs. As landlord, you cannot use the last month's rent as a security deposit for damage or cleaning costs. So a security deposit is your answer to many potential problems.

Be aware of your competition, however. If conditions favor the tenant in a slow market, then you may have to entirely eliminate the last month's rent or reduce the amount of security deposit. Pay attention to what your competition (other landlords) is doing. If it costs a tenant $300 or $400 more to rent your home than a comparable one, you may find yourself with a vacancy problem unless you reduce your move-in fees.

It is also a good practice to give your tenants a written policy statement as to what you expect of them with regard to the security deposit. Tell them what they must do and must not do if they expect to get back their full security deposit.

The tenant check-out list on next page is an excellent means of accomplishing this and also a good way to avoid arguments on how much money should be deducted from the security deposit. At the end of the lease, the security deposit must be returned (within two weeks) in full provided that all terms are met and the property is in proper condition.

Inspect The Property

Prior to a new occupancy, make an inspection tour of the property with the tenant. I recommend using a property acceptance form so that you can make a complete and accurate record of the condition of the property.

This checklist will be very instrumental in keeping peace between you and your tenants, because it is next to impossible to remember one year later what condition the property was in. When making your inspection, take notes on all categories. For instance, if a curtain is torn—say so. Describe the condition of painted walls with terms such as poor, fair, good, excellent. After your inspection, date the checklist and both you and the tenant sign it.

When your tenant moves, again inspect the property in his presence. Expect normal wear and tear, but if there are any major discrepancies, insist that your tenant be responsible. Any broken windows, door hinges, etc. should be paid for by the tenant. If you are holding a security deposit, the cost of repairs can come from it. Dirty floors, filthy ovens, etc. would be covered by the cleaning charge and/or the security deposit.

You should not have any arguments when you use the signed property acceptance form in conjunction with the tenant check-out list.

Unscheduled Inspections

Many landlords like to make unannounced property inspections during the course of the lease. I don't believe in this. If you use the recommended Lease-Rental Agreement (Form 105), you are not allowed to make inspections without "reasonable notice." An inspection—for no specific reason—will do nothing but damage the relationship between you and your tenant. If you know there are problems and you think that the tenant may be violating the lease, then go ahead and make your inspection. But an inspection for no reason at all is just plain harassment.

Tenant Check-Out List

- *KITCHEN*
  1 Clean refrigerator inside, outside, behind and underneath.
  2 Clean stove inside, outside, racks, broiler and top drip pans. Clean fan.
  3 Clean cabinets inside and outside. Remove all paper.
  4 Clean dishwasher inside and outside. Clean light fixtures.
  5 Clean floors—remove wax or shampoo carpet.

- *BATHROOM*
  1 Clean shower stalls, walls, chrome, fan, medicine cabinet, drawers, tub and toilet.
  2 Clean floors, baseboards, mirrors and light fixtures.

- *BEDROOMS AND LIVING ROOM*
  1. Clean all closets, doors, door tracks and baseboards.
  2. Vacuum rugs.

- *MISCELLANEOUS*
  1. Clean all windows inside and out. Dust screens.
  2. Clean and replace all light fixtures.
  3. Vacuum wall heater and air conditioner.
  4. Clean all baseboards and wood panelling, if any.
  5. Sweep and wash, if necessary, all balconies and/or patios.
  6. Remove all trash, clippings or debris from premises.
  7. Tenant will be responsible for any breakage.

Deposit Deductions

PAINTING: If needed and occupancy has been less than one year, the full charge will be deducted — over one year and less than two, the charge will be one-half. After two years — there will be no charge except for damage to walls.

CARPETS: For occupancy less than one year, the charge will be $25 for cleaning. For over one year, the charge will be one-half and over two years, no charge.

APPROXIMATE CHARGES FOR ITEMS NOT CLEANED

KITCHEN		PAINT	
Stove	10.00	Per wall	10.00
Dishwasher	5.00		
Stove hood	7.50	MISCELLANEOUS	
Refrigerator	5.00	Tracks of sliding	
Disposal	2.00	doors and closets	5.00
Cabinets	10.00		
Counters	5.00	FLOORS	
Wash Walls	20.00	Carpets	25.00
		Wax floors	10.00
BATHROOM			
Cabinets	5.00	WINDOWS	
Tub & Shower	10.00	Inside & out	5.00
Fixtures	5.00		
Wash Walls	10.00	YARD DEBRIS	
		(Each pick-up	
		truck load)	45.00

HOME MANAGEMENT SERVICES
PROPERTY ACCEPTANCE FORM

Address: _____

DESCRIPTION OF CONDITION

KITCHEN
doors _____
walls _____
ceiling _____
floor _____
stove _____
refrigerator _____
window and screen ____
curtain & rods _____
cupboards _____
drainboard _____
sink _____
electrical _____
other:

LIVINGROOM
doors _____
walls _____
ceiling _____
floors _____
carpets _____
window & screen _____
drapes & rods _____
electrical _____
other:

HALL
floors _____
doors _____
walls _____
ceiling _____
carpets _____
window & screen _____
drapes & rods _____
electrical _____
other:

BATHROOM ONE
doors _____
walls _____
ceiling _____
floor _____
toilet _____
basin _____
tub/shower _____
medicine cabinet ____
electrical _____
window & screen ____
other:

BATHROOM TWO
doors _____
walls _____
ceiling _____
floor _____
toilet _____.
basin _____
tub/shower _____
medicine cabinet ____
electrical _____
window & screen ____
other:

GARAGE
door _____
other:

YARD
front lawn _____
back lawn _____
trees _____
shrubs _____
other:

BEDROOM ONE
doors _____
walls _____
ceiling _____
floor _____
window & screen _____
curtain/drapes _____
closet _____
electrical _____
other:

BEDROOM TWO
doors _____
walls _____
ceiling _____
floors _____
window & screen _____
closet _____
curtain/drapes _____
closet _____
electrical _____
other:

BEDROOM THREE
doors _____
walls _____
ceiling _____
floors _____
window & screen _____
curtain/drapes _____
closet _____
electrical _____
other:

continued, over

Sample of a typical form for acceptance of description of condition of property. Reverse side lists names of Lessee, Lessor, date of acceptance; has additional space for other rooms, comments; signatures.

Repairs And The Tenant

Some so-called "slum-landlords" will milk their income properties and only make repairs when they are forced to do so. It is a completely different story with single-family home investments. Your eventual profit depends upon the property always being in near perfect condition. I have recommended buying clean, well-kept homes that will attract top-flight tenants. Although you should not spend a great deal of time or money on repairs and improvement projects until just before you place the home for sale, you must be prepared to properly maintain your property. And your tenant is the key to success.

Be firm with each new tenant. Let him know that you expect him to properly care for the house by doing such normal things as fixing loose hinges, cutting and watering lawns on a regular basis, removing all debris, etc. Also insist that he notify you whenever there is a significant problem with the property. After you are told of a problem, correct it promptly. If the problem was caused by the tenant—like a jammed garbage disposal because of improper use—you must insist that he call a repairman and pay the bill.

The proper time to *train* your tenant is when you and he are signing the lease or rental documents. Politely point out the small print in the agreement (such as the maintenance, repairs or alterations section in the sample lease form 105) which says the "tenant shall be responsible for all repairs required for exposed plumbing or electrical wiring and for damages caused by his negligence," etc.

Tell him that you will not be responsible for cosmetic changes such as a new paint job just because their furniture goes better with green walls than white walls. If you can determine in advance just what you will do and will not do, your life as a landlord will be much easier.

Routine maintenance—like tree trimming, painting and emergency repairs can be handled in any one of four ways. Each method should be considered. They are:

1. *Yourself:* If you are capable of most repairs and maintenance chores and if you have the time then there is no one better. The time you put in will pay extra dividends down the road.

2. *Hired Help:* You can hire all the work done by experts. This can include property management. This method costs you more, of course. But if you are short on either time or ability, it may be a necessity. It is better to pay a little extra than to be deprived of rental homes.

3.   *Tenant:* A knowledgeable tenant can perform many chores for you at a small reduction in rent. I have had many tenants ask me if they can paint a bedroom or bathroom and if I will buy the paint. I almost always agree to this proposition — provided that they meet my quality standards and use a light or off-white paint color.

4.   *Don't Do It:* Necessary repairs, of course, cannot be put off. But many maintenance projects like painting can be delayed. You may be thinking of selling the home in another year, in which case just prior to resale is the proper time to spend a few dollars on improvements.

A word of warning. Under many state housing laws and most local codes, the landlord is required to maintain rental property in a sound structural condition. This specifically includes the roof, plumbing and heating facilities. If you refuse or delay in making needed repairs, the tenant can withhold rent payments or hire someone to do the work and deduct the cost from your next month's rent. The tenant cannot do this for minor problems, however. The problem must be of a significant nature and the tenant must show the landlord delayed or refused repairs, under a recent decision of the California Supreme Court (Green vs. Superior Court; January 15, 1974). The best advice I can give is don't let yourself ever get into this position, because there is no need to.

You Need A Good Accounting System

Record keeping is very important! Not only do you need accurate records of all your income and disbursements but you will also need these records to provide Uncle Sam with correct tax information. It isn't hard to keep these records. I use a simple three-in-one system that does not take me more than an hour each month for my properties.

My system is comprised of one checkbook and register. The bank calls it the "Executive Deluxe." All it is is a checkbook with three checks per page which are opposite the register. The register allows me to do all my bookkeeping. Here I record all rents paid plus all disbursements made. I keep all repair receipts in a separate pouch. At the end of the year I tally up all my income and expenses for each home and take them to my accountant who then prepares a nice tax loss for my yearly returns.

Sample of an easy record keeping system

CHECK NO.	DATE	CHECK ISSUED TO / or Received	IN PAYMENT OF	AMOUNT OF CHECK	✓	DATE OF DEPOSIT	AMOUNT OF DEPOSIT →	BALANCE
			BALANCE BROUGHT FORWARD →					145 15
	11/2/74	John Smith	Strand Rent			11/2	300 00	445 15
	11/2	William Arnold	Merian Rent			11/2	260 00	705 15
	11/4	James Johnson	Eastgate Rent			11/4	275 00	980 15
	11/4	Judy Maddy	Gregory Rent			11/4	310 00	1,290 15
	11/6	Tom Baker	May Ct. Rent			11/6	300 00	1,590 15
263	11/6	ABC Mortgage Co.	Strand Mortgage	250 60				
264	11/6	Bank of Pleasant Hill	Merian "	265 00				
265	11/6	ABC Mortgage Co.	Eastgate "	240 00				
266	11/6	Smith Mortgage Co.	Gregory "	292 00				
267	11/6	Bank of Pleasant Hill	May Ct. "	250 00				293 15
	11/7	David Jones	Main St. Rent			11/8	260 00	553 15
			(includes $10 late ch)					
268	11/8	Smith Mortgage Co.	Main St. Mortgage	220 00				333 15
269	11/8	Mrs. Betty Anderson	May 2nd paym.	35 00				
270	11/8	Bills Plumbing Service	Eastgate-leak	50 00				248 15
271	11/12	Jims Fixit Shop	Strand - Repair	20 00				228 15
	12/1/74	John Smith	Strand Rent			12/2	300 00	528 15
	12/2	William Arnold	Merian Rent			12/2	260 00	788 15

What Should The Rent Be?

The amount of rent you charge for your property should be determined by what you can get more than what you need to make all the figures work, so you can have a cash flow.

And what you can get is the same thing as market value—the top rental price your property can get in open competition with other properties. If your property is in good condition it will bring considerably more dollars than a similar home which is run down. Get to know rental prices in your area. Ask Realtors and other rental owners what rents they are getting.

You must become familiar with rental prices because the biggest potential problem you face is having your property overpriced. If you are asking $20 more per month than others are for similar properties, you will be the loser. Renters shop around for the best bargain. It is seldom that a landlord catches a tenant who will pay more than market value. Most likely an overpriced property will mean that you will have a month or more vacancy. And there is no need for a vacancy. In the long run it will pay to price your homes correctly—or even a little low.

Vacancy Factor

Vacancy allowances are absolutely necessary when considering commercial or multi-unit investment property. Without a vacancy factor ranging between 2 and 10 per cent, you cannot properly appraise or determine actual gross income.

With single family property, however, a vacancy factor is a different matter. If you are the conservative type, you might want to recognize that you could lose 5 per cent of your projected yearly income due to vacancies. This awareness might save you from getting in over your head.

For the most part, however, I recommend ignoring the vacancy factor for residential property investments. If you own just two or three rentals, you should seldom have a vacancy problem. Department of Commerce figures show that the vacancy rate for apartment units was 5.4 per cent in the fourth quarter of 1975, whereas the single family home vacancy rate for the same quarter was only 1.2 per cent, a level which has been fairly steady for the last three years.

As stated before, you should not have a serious vacancy problem if you do three things: 1) Maintain a clean, well-cared-for rental; 2) begin showing the property 30 days prior to previous tenant's leaving; and 3) realistically price your rental at or below market value.

You are most likely going to have a vacancy either right after you buy a property or if you have an uncooperative tenant that won't show the property while he is living in it. (See Chapter VI, Insist on Tenant Cooperation.)

Occasionally the time of the year or month will have an effect on renting property. You will find that few people are willing to move close to the Christmas holidays. Also more people want to move on the first or last day of the month than in the middle. This is due to either end-of-the-month paydays or because they must be out of a previous home or apartment at the end of the month.

There are many exceptions, of course, so don't slacken your efforts to obtain a tenant. As soon as you take title to a property or receive notice from a moving tenant, have your Realtor (or you) place a sign on the property and a small ad in the rental columns of your local newspaper. You might even want to place notices on bulletin boards of a nearby grocery store or large company.

In most communities rentals are very scarce. If you get socked with a long-term vacancy it will most likely be because you didn't get to work on obtaining a new tenant when you should have.

Using Your Realtor For Tenant Selection

Most investors I know personally select their own tenants, even though they use Realtor services for buying and selling. If you are knowledgeable and do not become emotionally involved, then it is a good idea to select your own tenants. A Realtor knows what he is doing but nobody but yourself will give each prospect the careful attention that is needed.

I select the majority of my tenants and I have yet to have a serious problem. At times tenants have been obtained through cooperating Realtors or a salesman in my own office. Some of these selections turned out to be not so good. You must be prepared to give your personal touch to each prospect — nobody else will do it for you. And if you are unable to take the time or if you tend to become too emotionally involved, then you must select a competent Realtor. You should also consider qualified property management if you find yourself in this latter category.

VI

Selling and Refinancing

To make money — I mean really big money — you must pyramid your original equities into bigger profits and then pyramid those returns into yet bigger gains.

This brings us to the fifth success factor — RETRIEVING YOUR PROFITS. Translated, this means cashing-in your chips without losing anything of real value — without being set back. Paying a large amount of taxes is a setback! Sure, you can't always avoid them, but to successfully retrieve your profits you should strive to avoid triggering any capital gain taxes whenever possible. (A complete explanation of capital gains can be found on page 83.)

Retrieving your profits can be accomplished in one of two ways . . . selling or refinancing. Here are the basic differences between the two methods:

When you sell a rental property that you have owned for over 12 months, according to today's tax laws you must pay a long-term capital gains tax on the profit made in the sale. This tax is applied to only one-half of the profit you realize, so it could be worse. And of course profit means all the money you made on the transaction over and above your acquisition costs, your capital improvement costs and your selling costs.

Throughout the next chapters I will cover in more detail ways that you can greatly reduce your capital gains taxes. They are basically simple — sell only when 1) you have no other choice; 2) are in the midst of a poor tax year so the extra income from the property sales will not affect you much; 3) when you can carry back the first mortgage or a large second so that your profits are distributed over several tax years or 4) early in the year so that you will have ample time to buy more properties which in turn will shield the gain on the property sold.

When You Should Refinance

There are many advantages to be gained by refinancing rather than selling a property. But each individual property has its own unique financial and physical makeup, so therefore you must carefully weigh the facts involved. Here are four factors (taxes, property condition, available lender and equity ratio) that you must consider.

1. *Taxes:* Refinancing does not eliminate capital gains taxes but it does DEFER them until you have enough tax shelter for adequate protection. In other words, you can refinance a property now . . . and 10 years from now . . . and never pay any federal taxes. Many people just keep refinancing a property until the day they die—completely beating the tax collector in their lifetime. Only death or sale will bring on the tax collector.

If you have a desire to take an extended around-the-world vacation someday, then here is a suggestion that might make it possible. Let's assume that you own several rentals and have enough tax shelter to protect nearly $40,000 worth of income. By planning in advance you could take a leave of absence from your work for an entire calender year. Your salary, of course, will be gone. But this is the year that you could sell a rental home and retrieve $40,000 (for your trip) and completely avoid paying any income taxes.

2. *Property Condition:* As I pointed out before, to pyramid profits to bigger and better gains, you must either sell or refinance. (A third technique—trading—is only a remote possibility with single family homes.) If your tax situation is a major hurdle, then you are probably left with only one real choice—refinancing. Your second important consideration will be the condition of the property.

In spite of tax problems, I will personally sell a home, rather than refinance, if the property is in need of too many repairs. This is especially the case if I foresee a new $2,000 roof in the next 3 or 4 years. But if I am particularly fond of a property and its neighborhood, then I will refinance it and allow for enough cash to buy two more homes.

The following Refinancing Checklist will help you decide whether to sell or refinance a property. The theory is simple: If you will need to spend more on a home in the next 5 years than you will have to pay in capital gains taxes, then you will probably be better off *selling* rather than refinancing.

3. *Available Lender:* If the loan on your rental property is an FHA or GI then you are completely free to shop for the best new refinance loan available. This is because these loans do not contain

prepayment penalties. But if you have a conventional loan there is an excellent chance that you have a big prepayment penalty. This could be as much as one-half year's interest or in dollars well over $1,000.

When you have a conventional loan you must first determine what the prepayment penalty will amount to. Check your mortgage or trust deed or make a call to your lender. This prepayment penalty can usually be fully eliminated if you refinance with the same lender that has the mortgage on your rental home. Policies do vary from lender to lender, however. Find out if they will waive the penalty and what interest rate and loan costs they will charge.

Your second step is to contact other lenders to find out what their rates will be. Keep in mind that almost all conventional money will require prepayment penalties while FHA and GI refinancing will require you to pay loan discount points, because when you refinance you must pay all normal *SELLER* and *BUYER* costs just as if the home were being sold.

If all these costs are too high and if current interest rates are exceptionally high, then you might consider either waiting or selling instead of refinancing. Here's another fact to keep in mind: nearly all conventional lenders will charge at least ¼ per cent more interest on a refinance than they would for a buyer who intends to occupy the property.

4. *Equity Ratio:* There are many advantages to refinancing. But to make it worthwhile you must compare your total costs (i.e., prepayment penalty, new loan charges, etc.) against what you would save by not paying capital gains taxes. But that isn't enough! You must also compare the costs against what you expect to gain in the refinance. Do you really have enough equity to justify the expenses? Will you be able to buy at least two more properties with the cash you get?

Whether you use conventional or government insured refinancing, you will always be required to pay a larger down payment than if you were buying the home for the first time. Of course, you don't put the money down in cash because you already have it as equity. Many conventional lenders, for instance, will require the refinanced home to have 25 per cent equity rather than 20 per cent. So if your property is appraised at $40,000 and if your loan is $25,000 the most you could expect on a refinance is $5,000 (25 per cent equity equals $10,000 in this case) before expenses. And your expenses might well be $3,000 on a $40,000 refinance. Obviously this is not enough equity to make refinancing worthwhile. Now if the current loan in this example was only $15,000 then refinancing would make sense.

REFINANCING CHECKLIST

(Use this checklist to determine feasibility of refinancing
as opposed to selling a property.)

Estimated Selling Expenses

1. *Capital Gains Taxes:* To compute, base dollar figure on your
current tax bracket. (i.e., if you are in the 25% tax bracket,
then substract 25% from the taxable profit which is basically
half of the total profit after subtracting your original sales
price, selling expenses and capital improvements. See the
following chapter on taxes. . . . . $_____

2. *Repairs Necessary to Sell Home:*
(i.e., termite repairs, new carpeting, etc.) . . . . $_____

3. *Sales Commission* . . . . $_____

4. *Closing and Settlement Charges:* (i.e., pre-payment charges,
interest charges, loan discount points, etc.) . . . . . . $_____

Total Estimated Selling Costs $_____

Estimated Refinancing Charges

1. *Charges that a Seller Would Normally Have:* (i.e., loan
discount points, pre-payment penalty, interest, etc.) . . . $_____

2. *Charges that a Buyer Would Normally Have:* (i.e. new loan
fee, title and/or escrow, appraisal fee, credit fee, recording
charges, etc.) . . . . $_____

3. *Effects of Possible Higher Interest Rates:* (i.e., if lender
charges ¼ per cent or more in interest rates what would
the net results be for a five year period compared against
a purchase made at the lower rate? Note: The difference
between a 30-year 9 per cent and a 9¼ per cent loan is
.18¢ per thousand.) . . . . $_____

4. *Any Repairs that Lender May Require to Refinance*
(i.e., a lender may require certain repairs—like replacing
worn-out carpeting—prior to completing the refinance) . . $_____

Total Estimated Refinancing Costs $_____

The estimated refinancing costs should be considerably lower than the
estimated selling costs, or it may not be worthwhile to refinance.

Other Reasons For Refinancing

Refinancing can be used in many ways, from paying off debts to obtaining capital to get you started on your own investment program. In many states you may refinance your personal residence as often as you would like and for whatever reason. But in other states, like Texas, there is a Homestead Law which prevents anyone from refinancing their personal residence.

One of my favorite ways of refinancing is what I call a "five-year plan." For instance, I would buy a rental now with a 10 per cent down payment and have the seller carry back a 10 per cent interest only second deed of trust. In five years, just before the second is due and payable, I will refinance the home. If appreciation rates continue at 10 per cent or better, not only will I have enough equity to pay off the second but I will have enough money left over to start the buying process all over again.

Lease Option Contract

Before I give you sound professional techniques for selling your property, I am going to give you a shortcut that should save you a lot of time and money. This simple but often overlooked selling method is the "lease option contract."

With high appreciation rates, I recommend that you keep each property at least four years and no longer than five years. Let's assume that you are now three years along with your first home and you want to sell in one more year. If your present tenants are staying on, ask them if they would like a lease option. If they are not interested and the property is vacant or soon to be vacant, place a lease-option ad in the newspaper instead of the regular "For Lease" ad.

Basically, a lease option contract gives the tenant (prospective buyer) the chance to buy the property at a later date. And the price he will pay is the fair market value of the home at the end of one year — not the value at the time the least option is signed. If today's value is $30,000, you might estimate a $33,000 sale price for one year into the future. A better way, however, is to write into your agreement the following clause: "The purchase price shall be determined by an independent appraisal ordered after (date one month before expected close of escrow)."

An extremely important point is that with a traditional option the prospective buyer pays cash for the privilege of keeping the property available to him. But with the lease-option, the procedure is just the opposite. You must pay the buyer! Allow up to $50 per month of the rent to be applied towards the purchase price or closing costs. After one year the tenant can have $600 saved to apply toward the purchase. And if the tenant decides not to purchase, you keep the $600. With that amount of money at stake the odds are strong he will complete the sale. And when the sale is made, the lease-option contract will save a lot of dollars that you would have had to spend on painting, carpeting, etc.

You can obtain lease-option forms from Professional Publishing Corporation. They are called "Residential Lease with Option to Purchase" Form 106. (Box 4187, San Rafael, Calif. 94903)

Fix It Up—A Little

Odds are good that you will be successful in obtaining a purchaser with a lease option contract. But if it doesn't work out that way be prepared to spend some money (but not too much) to fix up the home.

Foremost, you will want to have a clean, freshly painted home with good floors. If you have followed all the guidelines previously set out, you should (because of excellent tenants) have a clean property that is not too badly in need of paint.

If the home will not show well to a buyer—then make corrections. You can save a lot of money by doing the work yourself or you can save a fairly substantial amount of money by hiring the work done. I have a list of several "moon-lighters"; painters, handymen, etc. who not only do an expert job but charge very little in comparison to union craftsmen.

I mentioned three important areas that you must have looking good—the wall paint, floors and overall cleanliness. I don't mean that you should overlook other items such as broken windows, overgrown shrubs, missing switches, etc. You must, however, remember that a buyer often makes his decision within the first three minutes of stepping into the home. So you must be prepared by having everything the prospective buyer sees at first glance in tip-top shape. Keep this in mind and follow priorities in preparing your property for sale.

Floor conditions are vital. If you have worn or dull wall to wall carpeting—replace it. If the hardwood floors are scratched and dull—refinish them. Floors and floor coverings are important. Give serious consideration to carpeting. It need not be expensive. Shop around to find out where you can get your best wholesale buys. I always buy "seconds" (carpeting that comes from the mills with minor defects). Not only can you receive as much as a 50 per cent discount on "seconds" but you probably will not be able to even find the defects.

A word of warning! Keep your paint and carpeting colors neutral or at least popular. Buy off-white or very light colors for paint and light gold or green for carpeting. Save any decorating flairs you might have for your own residence. Most people don't like purple walls and fire engine red carpeting.

Use Realtor Services

When it comes time to sell your home you have two courses of action available. One is to hire a competent Realtor and the other is to sell it yourself "By Owner." I recommend using a Realtor.

It has been proven a thousand times over that when a seller tries to save a commission by doing it himself, he usually fails. There are too many pitfalls and, besides, a buyer who buys directly from an owner is also trying to save the commission. At best a compromise is reached. In the long run you will probably make more money with a Realtor than without one.

Here's an important inside tip I'll pass along to you. Not *all* Realtors are hardworking, honest and professional! Shop around for one who is. Give him or her all of your business. Develop a working relationship.

By exclusively using one person and one firm you can expect above-board service and extra help. Level with the agent. Tell him that you expect to do all of your business through him, except for those instances where you find a low assumption direct from the owner or where you sell a home on a lease-option contract. Even then it might be wise to pay your Realtor a fee to handle the technical side of your transactions.

Don't be afraid to ask your agent to recommend a good handyman or to tell you where to find carpeting "seconds." A good relationship is a two-way proposition that will pay big dividends for both you and your Realtor.

Insist On Tenant Cooperation

In Chapter V, I stressed the importance of a good tenant-landlord relationship. It is very important that good relationships be maintained through close of escrow. The lease-rental agreement form 105 gives you the right to show the property to prospective tenants or purchasers. But it goes deeper than just the right to show. You will need the tenant's complete and cheerful cooperation.

Nothing is worse than tenants who will only let you show the property from 1 to 4 p.m. on Tuesday and Thursday. And when you do show it, they are quick to point out the leaky roof and busy street traffic. Ask your tenants to show the property at any reasonable hour and to step aside when the customer is in the home. It is your job—or your Realtor's—to explain any leaky roofs.

It is also important to have your tenants keep the home as clean as possible and to allow a key for the home to be placed in a Realtor's lockbox. A good relationship is possible if, from the very beginning, you select the proper tenants and if you always treat them fairly.

There will come a time, however, when you will not receive the tenant's cooperation. Or perhaps the tenants are such poor housekeepers that prospective buyers leave the property holding their nose. If this happens to you—kick them out (with a proper notice in writing) before you try to show the property.

The Price Must Be Right

If your property is worth $40,000 and you have an asking price of $42,000—you are going to lose money. Conversely, if you are asking $38,000 you are also going to lose money. In the first example you will lose money because the odds are high that you will have a vacant home for a few months until you decide to reduce or to accept the $40,000 price.

The point I am making is simple. Find out the true market value of your property—and then price it at market value. In most cases you can be within $1,000 of true market value. No intelligent buyer will pay more for a property than what it is worth.

Market value can be determined most accurately by a professional appraiser and often accurately by your personal Realtor. I stress "your personal Realtor" because if you ask three real estate salesmen for their opinion of value you may get three different answers, all colored by the hope that they can outbid any competition and thus receive a listing.

You can get a fairly accurate picture of market value yourself by locating three identical or at least somewhat similar properties to yours that have sold in the past six months in the same area. Use only final sales prices. Pay little attention to asking prices and pay no attention at all to rumors. After a rumor gets started and passed between 10 neighbors a price can balloon several thousand dollars.

Reselling FHA And GI

FHA and GI loans are a mixed bag for the property investor. Without these loans it would be difficult for the small investor to maintain a portfolio of single family homes. They are just about the only loans that you can assume without a prepayment penalty for the seller and without an increase in interest or qualification problems for the buyer. For these reasons, I like them.

But when it comes to selling, FHA and GI loans are another story. If it is at all possible you should avoid selling to a buyer by means of a new FHA or GI. Sell on conventional loan terms whenever possible. Conventional loans are available with as little as 5 and 10 per cent down payment to owner-occupant buyers. Use FHA or GI financing only when you must. There are six reasons why I don't like to resell FHA or GI. They are:

1. *Slow:* Nothing is slower. During the busiest time of year it often takes two or three months to process the loans.

2. *Appraisals:* FHA and the Veterans Administration each have their own appraisers. You often wait two or three weeks for their valuation and then there is a good chance the value will not be correct. I recently ordered an FHA appraisal for a client on a home that should sell for $33,000. The appraisal was $29,500. This situation, unfortunately, is quite common.

3. *Loan Discount Points:* You, the seller, must pay loan discount points which may range from 0 to 8. If points are high you can lose a lot of money. And it is often difficult to know what points will be. They may be just "2" today, but if the government lowers the interest rate, these points could jump to "6" and you will have to pay the higher amount.

4. *Conditions:* Although GI appraisals do not usually contain conditions, FHA appraisals are well known for requiring many things to be replaced or repaired prior to closing. On the $29,500 FHA appraisal referred to, there was also a condition requiring a partial new roof. The roof, however, was only five years old and in near perfect condition.

5. *Closing Costs:* Don't think for a moment that a GI loan will be better because their appraisals may not have costly conditions. The Veterans Administration " protects" their GI buyers by making it mandatory that many closing costs (like escrow charges) be paid by the seller. Both GI and, to a lesser degree, FHA will cost you more money at closing than a conventional sale.

6. *Arbitrary:* Bureaucrats run both programs. When you have a problem they will not talk to the seller, seldom to the Realtor, and hardly ever to the lender. They are arbitrary and usually uncooperative. For instance, if you have a potential GI buyer, but you are not sure whether he can qualify because of a particular problem, it is only logical to call the VA and ask what to do. But the stock answer I usually get (and lenders and I have tried more than once) is "We cannot tell you, sir, you will have to submit the package." So we all lose time and money by submitting the package and waiting two or three months for the answers.

The preceding problems demonstrate many of the obstacles you can expect to face when selling with FHA or GI terms. You will find, however, that many times you cannot avoid selling with government terms. If loan discount points are low and if FHA and GI money is the best around at the time—you don't have much choice. Ask your Realtor—he will know when times are best in your market area to sell via government financing.

When you do sell your property with government terms, here are two important considerations to keep in mind. First, be sure to limit the amount of discount points you will pay. Put it in writing in your listing agreement and sales contract. If the points go higher than three or four you might consider holding your property off the market for a period of time.

Secondly, make sure your prospective buyer is well qualified. If his gross income to total house payment (principle, interest, taxes and insurance) ratio is at least 3½ to 1 and if his credit rating appears strong then there will be an excellent chance that he will be approved for the loan. Take out an insurance policy too! Write on your sales contract that "Buyer's credit and loan package are to be approved by lender within 10 working days or this contract is null and void." This statement isn't a complete guarantee but I have found that it eliminates many unqualified buyers in 10 days rather than waiting two months for eventual rejection by FHA or VA.

VII

Taxes

Taxes can eat you alive. But you can do something about them. A real estate investment portfolio can not only reduce your taxes but can eventually eliminate all state and federal income taxes.

A valued friend and associate taught me several years ago that tax shelters were just as much for the little guy as the big guy. He earned as much money selling real estate as he needed for his family, and he didn't pay one cent in income tax. His secret, of course, was the rental properties that he owned. He is now semi-retired, at age 45, and living in Oregon. He was a good salesman—not a great one—but he was a wise investor.

I am writing this chapter to give you some understanding of the tax problems and tax breaks you can expect with your investment portfolio. I do not mean you should not get counseling from your accountant or tax man.

Tax Time Blues

In late winter or early spring most of us begin to wrestle with form 1040, a clear indication that "the tax man cometh."

Your task will be a lot simpler at tax time if you have kept complete records of all monies spent in the "three-in-one" check writing system as outlined in Chapter V. All receipts for monies spent should also be kept together in a handy spot.

There are two types of allowed deductions. The first category is capital expenses which are usually large items such as a new roof or a new range and oven. They also include loan discount points which are treated as prepaid interest. Because these expenses are for items over a period of time, they must be depreciated (spread over a certain number of years).

All other expenses are deducted in the year they occur. (To help simplify your returns, I recommend that you obtain form 4831 [Rental Income] as it will make your job a lot easier if you own two or more properties.) Following is a partial list of allowed expenses:

Advertising	Legal and accounting
Auto and travel	Management fees
Cleaning	Office supplies
Commissions paid	Repairs (to be listed)
Gardening	Supplies
Insurance	Taxes and licenses
Interest	Telephone and utilities

Depreciation

The word "depreciation" is the opposite of the word "appreciation." Appreciation signifies a gain in value for your property. Depreciation, on the other hand, refers to a loss in value caused by deterioration and/or obsolescence. We will ignore this definition of depreciation, however.

For our purposes, the word "depreciation" will be defined as the spreading of the cost of an income-producing property over the life of the property. It is a "book entry" which does not represent any loss in market value of the property.

You must establish three things in order to compute your "depreciation deduction." They are your cost or other tax basis; the useful life of the property; and the method of depreciation you intend to use.

1. *Cost or other tax basis:* This figure is basically the sum of the costs for the property at the time of purchase. It would include your cash down payment, first trust deed, second trust deed if any, and other miscellaneous acquisition costs. All considered, your figures might add up to $30,440 on a $30,000 purchase. This $30,440 will be "locked in" as your cost basis.

2. *Useful Life:* Depreciation cannot be computed without first determining the useful life of the property. Land (the lot your rental property is on) cannot be depreciated since land lasts forever. Useful life is the number of years which the property may reasonably be expected to be useful to the taxpayer. The useful life is only an estimate, but it must be reasonable. The Internal Revenue code includes a guideline for determining useful life. They recommend 45 years for dwellings. Because most of my own rentals are 15 to 25 years old, I have success-

fully used a 30-year term. Be sure and consult with your tax man, because each situation is different.

3.   *Method of Depreciation:* There are three basic methods of depreciation, which are: Straight Line; Sum of the Years — Digits; and Declining Balance. Declining Balance method is broken down into 200 per cent (double the straight-line); 150 per cent and 125 per cent.

To simplify an otherwise confusing situation, all you must remember is that with used residential property you can apply only two of the methods. They are the straight line and the 125 per cent declining balance methods.

The straight line method is probably used more often because it is the easiest. Using this method, you deduct the cost of the property equally over its useful life. Thus the amount of depreciation deduction is the same the first year as it is the last. I personally avoid the 125 per cent declining balance method because of "Recapture," which I will explain shortly.

Here is an example of how straight line depreciation is used with a $30,000 cost basis:

$$
\begin{array}{ll}
\text{Original Cost} & \$30,000 \\
\text{less land} & -6,000 \\
\hline
& \$24,000
\end{array}
$$

We now have $24,000 to be depreciated for a term of 30 years. This represents 3 1/3 per cent each year.

$$
\begin{array}{r}
\$24,000 \\
\times\ .033 \\
\hline
\$792.00
\end{array}
$$

$792 is your depreciation figure which you may now deduct from your income taxes provided that your property expense and income totals come out to "0".

Capital Gains

Income is either "ordinary" or "capital gains." Ordinary income is taxed at 100 percent, whereas long term capital gains (investments held 12 months or longer) are taxed at only 50 per cent. A capital gain is the profit made on the sale or exchange of a capital asset or a non-capital asset that is treated as such under the provisions of Internal Revenue Code 1231.

While capital gains give us a tax break, they also cause a problem. Rental homes do not automatically qualify for capital gains. This hits the real estate license holders the hardest. Depreciable property used in a taxpayer's trade or business as inventory is not considered a capital asset. When you sell depreciable property at a profit, you will probably find that some or all of the profit will be taxed as ordinary income rather than capital gain under the so-called "depreciation recapture" rule. These rules are fairly complicated.

Generally speaking, the individual investor who occasionally buys a rental and then sells it a few years later for a profit, has a long-term capital gain. The courts themselves often disagree on what is correct. This is one area where tax advice from a professional is a must.

Capital gain is computed by subtracting your adjusted cost basis from the selling price less the selling expenses of the property. The adjusted basis of the property is the original cost (cost basis) plus cost of capital improvements less depreciation allowed since acquisition.

Depreciation Recapture

The recapture rules for real property are very complicated. They generally apply if accelerated depreciation has been deducted.

The Tax Reform Act of 1969 reduced the tax benefit opportunities of depreciable real estate by allowing less accelerated depreciation and recapturing 100 per cent of all accelerated depreciation after 1969.

What the rules mean in simple terms is that any gain you make on depreciation deductions is now treated as capital gains. Thus, if you have declared $5,000 in deductions over a five-year period, then this amount is subject to capital gains tax ($2,500 being exempt, of course). This rule applies only to property bought after July 24, 1969.

This same Tax Reform Act also states that any excess depreciation taken will be recaptured as ordinary income—not capital gains. Excess depreciation is generally considered the difference between the amount actually deducted by an accelerated method and the amount that would have been deducted under the straight line method.

All considered, even with the new tax rules, the depreciation benefits of single family home rentals are still very worthwhile to your investment program.

1976 Tax Reform Law

In the name of tax equity, simplification and economic growth, Congress in 1976 passed a new tax bill. But from the investor's viewpoint the new tax reform act only means more complicated procedures and higher taxes.

Of particular interest to the investor who owns several properties is the section called "Limitation on Interest Deduction."Prior to the new bill, the allowed deduction was $25,000 for married taxpayers; now it is only $10,000.

Before we get into some of the ramifications of this new law, let me point out that most investors will not even have to worry about it! You will only have problems if your rental income far exceeds your interest deductions.

Basically, the new law means that you are only allowed to deduct from your taxes $10,000 in *excess* interest, which is interest from all investment sources, real estate or otherwise. For example, if you own several rentals that have combined interest deductions (the interest you pay on each mortgage loan) of $8,000 and a net rental income of $7,000 then you would have only $1,000 of what is called excessive interest deductions. And that amount would fall well within the limits of $10,000, so you would have no problem. And even if you did exceed $10,000 you could carry over the unused balance to other tax years until it was used up.

If a person is close to the $10,000 limit he then must consider the following test: If a property's expenses (everything but taxes, interest and depreciation) exceeds 15 per cent of the gross rental income, then it is treated as a "business" property and it is then exempt from the Limitation on Interest Deduction section. Expenses would include insurance, maintenance and repairs, management fees, advertising and transportations costs, etc.

However, if the expenses did not equal 15 per cent, then the property would be treated as "investment" property and would then be subject to the limitation. As this can be complicated, be sure and check with your tax firm.

VIII

Pyramiding
Your Equities

In the preceding chapters I have discussed most of the basic investment principles. Now let's put them to work. I am going to give you a plan that you can use to build a nice little fortune of about $300,000 over a 10- to 12-year period. To reach this goal you will need to understand the sixth success factor which is *BORROW-ING OTHER PEOPLE'S MONEY.*

There are both slower and faster ways of making money than the hypothetical formula which I am about to outline. Very few investors do things this exact way. Everyone has goals which fit their particular situation and wouldn't be practical for another investor. The program I am suggesting is a good plan to follow if you are earning between $12,000 and $22,000 a year. But don't hesitate to customize an investment plan that better suits you—there are literally hundreds of ways to make big money with single family rentals.

Starting On A Shoestring

The hypothetical investment plan which I am about to outline is designed for the investor with a minimum amount of capital available. The plan assumes purchasing a $30,000 property with $3,000 cash. But in actual practice an investor might need more to start, depending largely upon prices in his community. If the average home sells for $50,000 in your area then visualize yourself starting at that price.

A comparable home costing $25,276 in Austin, Texas, sells for $56,000 in Boston, according to figures released in March, 1976 by the Employee Transfer Corporation.

Cities with the highest housing prices are Boston, Anchorage, Honolulu and the New York City area. Investors in these and other high-priced areas will obviously need a bigger initial cash outlay.

The lowest-priced homes are in Austin, Atlanta, Houston, Denver and Bakersfield, California. Investors in these communities might even get by with substantially less than $3,000 to start.

In addition to a minimum cash investment, for this shoestring program you will need to set aside a small portion of your income for up to six years.

Let's assume that your first purchase was a $30,000 home and that you have a taxable income of $16,000 a year for your family of four. This places you in Uncle Sam's 25 per cent tax bracket.

After talking with your tax adviser, you will probably discover that your newly acquired rental property will be depreciated for tax purposes at $24,000 (less $6,000 which represents the lot value) on a straight line basis for a term of 30 years. To keep things simple, let's ignore your tax "cost basis" in this and other examples. This purchase will give you an $800 a year deduction from your tax bill (3 1/3 per cent of the $24,000 value), provided that your total property income isn't greater than your total property expenses. For instance, if you have a positive cash flow and few repair expenses you may show a profit and then you wouldn't have the full $800 deduction. Odds are, however, that with a new rental you will have a negative cash flow and thus will receive the full $800 deduction (and even more if you have fairly high repair bills).

Because you are in the 25 per cent tax bracket, the above example will give you a $200 cash savings. Now that Uncle Sam does not get to claim the $200, take it and put it into a bank or savings and loan account. Even if you earn only 5 per cent on the $200, at the end of two years you will have saved nearly $430 to go towards your second purchase.

In addition to your tax saving, I am asking you to set aside another $50 each month. If you do this faithfully, you will save another $1,264 by the end of two years. If you can afford to set $100 a month aside, you can increase this amount to $2,529. You can even do better, because you don't have to settle for just 5 per cent interest. Ask your bank or savings and loan about time certificate deposits. By placing amounts of $1,000 or more in special accounts for a set period of time (six months or one year) you will receive a much higher interest rate.

Using the two methods which I have outlined ($50 a month and your tax savings) you will have about $1,700 available for your second purchase. Most likely you will not find a property for just $1,700 cash to loan. But two other money sources are available to you. Both of these sources use the sixth success factor of BORROWING OTHER PEOPLE'S MONEY.

Second Mortgages

If you are earning $100,000 a year, then you will probably not need to borrow more money. (However, many people in the $100,000 a year bracket are earning this income because they are successfully using the principle of "Borrowing Other People's Money.") If you are like most people, however, the proper use of seconds is essential. I have used this technique several times and would not be where I am today if I didn't master seconds. Simply explained, a second deed of trust (or mortgage) is a legal instrument used to borrow someone else's money with a loan secured by property you own.

I am assuming that in preparing for your second purchase you find that $1,700 is not enough money to buy the property you want. You then have two choices.

Your first choice is to give the seller a note and second deed of trust for the amount of money you are short. This is called a "purchase money" second and is secured by the property you are buying. The seller advances you the money which you in turn give back to him. It is a paper transaction. There is an excellent chance, however, that the seller will need all of his equity and will not carry the second. If this happens you must now go to the second choice.

Your second choice is to take back a note and second secured by the home you bought two years ago. This choice is the best possibility because you have more than one source to obtain the money from. More on this later.

With either example, be prepared to pay the top legal interest rate in your state. In most states this rate is 10 per cent per annum. You can always offer to pay less, but in most cases you will probably have to pay the top rate.

Your costs for each $1,000 of a 10 per cent amortized second with a one-year due date is $87.92 per month. An amortized loan is one that is completely paid off, interest and principal, by a series of regular payments that are equal or nearly equal. Obviously, if you are on a budget an extra payment of $87.92 is out of the question. But there are many ways to handle this problem.

An amortized loan is okay for our purposes but only if you can arrange terms for a period of four or five years. A $1,000 amortized loan at 10 per cent and paid in five years is only $21.25 per month. A few years make quite a difference.

The best way to go, however, is to obtain an interest only loan for a five-year period. At 10 per cent interest this loan will cost you only $8.34 per thousand dollars. At the end of five years you will have a balloon payment of $1,000, the face amount of the note. This makes for good leverage, too, because in five years you will pay only a little over $500 (per each $1,000) in interest whereas the property will increase in value several thousands of dollars. The five-year terms are excellent, too, because you will want to sell the home before five years so that you can expand your equity from this home into three more.

As you can see, it is often necessary to raise extra cash by borrowing money with a note and second deed of trust secured by either the home you are buying or the one you already own. The latter choice is the most practical because you can obtain the money from any source. The sources would include relatives, friends, business acquaintances or so-called "hard money" lenders.

Another reason for this choice is that your first rental, now yours for two years, can better carry the burden because after a few years you should have a positive cash flow. For example, the home you bought two years ago for $30,000 should now have a value of $36,300 due to a 10 per cent appreciation each year. It should also be commanding a rent figure now between $20 and $30 more than the amount of your original lease.

Beware of "hard money" seconds, however. A hard money second is money obtained from a dealer who earns his living by lending money furnished by investors. Not only will the dealer charge the highest interest rates allowable, but the loan will cost you an extra 15 to 25 per cent in loan fees (the dealer's commission, prepayment charges, appraisal fees, credit report, etc.).

Hard money is a legitimate source but it should be avoided if at all possible. Always think ahead and you will be able to bypass hard money loans. Before you begin your search for a property, start looking for alternative sources. There are literally hundreds of other possibilities, including friends, relatives, credit union, your Realtor, etc.

If you would like more information on this important subject, I have written a book called "How to Grow a Moneytree, the magical book of making big money with second mortgages." You'll find an order blank in the back of this book.

Buying Your Second Property

Looking into the future can be risky business. It is hard to say whether property in your area will appreciate at 5 per cent . . . or 10 per cent . . . or 15 per cent. With an appreciation rate in 1977 which in some areas exceeded 20 per cent, it may be safe to assume that our guideline of a 10 per cent increase could possibly be conservative.

According to a study prepared by the U.S. League of Savings

Associations, "the annual rate of inflation between September, 1973, and September, 1974, was 12.1 percent, as measured by the Consumer Price Index. If inflation continues at the same pace for the next 10 years, it will take $3.1337 in 1984 to buy $1 worth of merchandise at today's prices. For example, a $40,000 house will sell for $125,000 in 10 years."

Regardless of how high inflation is during the next 10 years, your investment program will be profitable. At a 10 per cent rate you should have over $300,000 in equities in about 11 years. At a higher rate you will make even more. At a lower rate, you will still make money but you will have to stay with the program, and each home, a little longer. The following "Appreciation Charts" illustrate the point.

APPRECIATION CHART A
6% Yearly Rate

Original Sale Price

TERM	*$25,000*	*$30,000*	*$35,000*	*$40,000*	*$45,000*
1 year	1,500	1,800	2,100	2,400	2,700
2 years	1,590	1,908	2,226	2,544	2,862
3 years	1,685	2,022	2,360	2,697	3,034
4 years	1,786	2,143	2,501	2,858	3,216
5 years	1,894	2,272	2,651	3,030	3,409
5 YEARS TOTAL VALUE	33,455	40,146	46,838	53,529	60,221

APPRECIATION CHART B
10% Yearly Rate

Original Sales Price

TERM	*$25,000*	*$30,000*	*$35,000*	*$40,000*	*$45,000*
1 year	2,500	3,000	3,500	4,000	4,500
2 years	2,750	3,300	3,850	4,400	4,950
3 years	3,025	3,630	4,235	4,840	5,445
4 years	3,327	3,993	4,658	5,324	5,989
5 years	3,660	4,392	5,124	5,856	6,588
5 YEARS TOTAL VALUE	40,262	48,315	56,367	64,420	72,472

It isn't the purpose of the above charts to show you why you should buy a $45,000 home instead of a $25,000 home. Nor should the charts be taken as a precise measure of yearly values. We may experience a 10 per cent growth rate one year, 6 per cent the next and 8 per cent the third year. The real purpose of these charts is to give you an idea of what can be expected in appreciation from one year to the next and, most importantly, to demonstrate that money can be made in rental properties regardless of the appreciation rates. When I bought my first rental in 1968 the recognized rate in my area was between 4 and 5 per cent. But I still made nearly 100 per cent return on my invested dollar the first year. Good leverage can make you money at any appreciation rate — even a zero growth rate.

Using a 10 per cent appreciation guideline, let's take a look at what has happened to your first purchase after two full years.

Purchase Price	$30,000
Value two years later	36,300
	$6,300 gain
Loan at time of purchase	27,000
Loan two years later*	26,500
	$500 gain
Present Value	36,300
Loan amount	26,500
Paper Equity	$9,800

* Amortized loans (which includes all FHA and GI's) pay more on principal and less on interest each succeeding month. Thus a typical loan that would include principal pay-down of $18.00 the first month would pay-down $22.00 a month after a few years. Each month 20 cents or so (depending on original loan amount) will go to principal instead of interest. Because of this I have simplified all the loan pay-down examples by using an arbitrary figure of $500 for two years.

The above figures show that in two years you have, on paper thus far, turned $3,000 into $9,800. You also have another $1,700 ready for your second purchase. You're still a long way away from having a big nest egg, but things begin to get interesting at this point. After all, in just two years you have turned $3,000 into almost $10,000 for over 100 per cent per year return on your invested dollar. Now go ahead and buy your second property.

With values climbing sky high each successive year, you will discover that you cannot find another property like your first for a mere $30,000. Your new purchase, we will assume, will cost you $36,000. And because of a higher price you will find that it will be necessry to pay $3,500 cash to the loan. Following the plan outlined, which calls for saving $50 per month plus your tax savings, you will be short of cash and therefore must obtain a 10 per cent second in the amount of $1,800. It might take you a few months and you might have a couple of offers rejected, but you will succeed in finding the right property.

Four Years Later

Once again we look into the crystal ball to see what is happening four years after your first purchase and two years after your second purchase. I use the phrase "crystal ball" not because this investment program isn't based upon sound principle, but to point out again that the second success factor of "appreciation" depends largely upon inflation — and inflation rates, although always upward, can vary.

FOUR YEARS GROWTH

- PURCHASE No. 1   Value . . . $43,600
  (after 4 years appreciation)

  Loan on Purchase No. 1   26,000
  (approx. another $500 paid)
                                      Paper Equity   17,600

- PURCHASE No. 2   Value . . . $43,560

  Loan on Purchase No. 2   32,000
                                        Paper Equity   11,560

Total Equities   29,160
less 1,800 second   1,800

paper net $27,360

As you did during the first two years, I am again asking that you put aside $50 per month plus the tax savings from each home. Assuming you are still in the 25 per cent tax bracket, you will now have approximately $2,300 available for purchase No. 3 — and No. 4 and 5. After four years we have reached the point where I am asking you to sell or refinance your first house and purchase three more, giving you a total of four houses. After four years of solid experience gained from your first two rentals, you are ready to fly. (To not complicate this hypothetical example I am going to stress selling over refinancing.)

Assuming you have now successfully sold and closed escrow on property No. 1 (refer to Chapter VI), you will have between $14,000 and $17,600 from that sale in your hands. The $3,600 difference is because if you have properly maintained your home (with the help of good tenants) and if you were able to sell it without the aid of your Realtor you might have close to the top dollar figure of $17,600.

For the sake of clarification, however, I will assume you now have the lower figure of $14,000 available. But now I must take away another $1,500 because Uncle Sam will want his share of capital gains.

Buying Numbers 3, 4 & 5

Armed now with $12,500 from your first sale and with $2,300 in savings you have $14,800 to spend on three houses. I am sure that at the end of four years it will be almost impossible to find $2,500-$3,000 FHA or GI assumptions. This is because of higher down payments required and the fact that homes will appreciate many more dollars at $43,000 than they did at $30,000.

Government programs and regulations will most likely be different four years from now. It is hard to say whether the government will make things easier or harder for investors in the future. If a GI buyer can still pay nothing down with limited closing costs then there is still hope for good $2,000 or $3,000 assumptions. But being realistic, I am suggesting paying up to $5,000 now for each purchase. I'll use that figure for the next three hypothetical houses you purchase.

Six Years Growth

The year is now 1982, or perhaps 1984, and you probably have a few more grey hairs. Your grey hairs are not caused by management problems; you're just six years older and several thousand dollars richer. Let's take a look at what has happened to your real estate holdings after six full years.

- Purchase No. 2 (after 4 years) value $52,707
  New Loan Balance   31,500
                                          21,207

      Less second deed of trust   1,800
      Paper Equity   19,407

- Property No. 3 (purchase price)   43,500
  Value 2 years later   52,635

      Original Loan $38,500
      New Loan Balance   38,000
      Paper Equity   14,635

- Properties No. 4 & 5   14,635
  (same as property No. 2)   14,635
                                         $43,905

At the end of six years you now own four rental properties and you have paper equities of $43,905 for your three latest acquisitions plus $1,407 on your second property for a grand total of $63,312.

For the sake of explanation, I have assumed that your last three purchases were all identical properties that you were able to buy at the identical price of $43,500. Of course, it will never happen that way. Most likely you would end up with purchase prices something like $39,000; $43,000 and $47,500 but averaging about $43,500. I have also assumed that your three purchases were made without the need of any second deeds of trust, although in reality you may have had to obtain a small second on one of the purchases. But with $5,000 cash you should have been able to find quality homes in that price range with the proper loan assumption figures.

More On Inflation

Your single family home investment program will certainly be affected by continued home value appreciation. And appreciation is a product of inflation. You can see what inflation does! While it eats into the value of your dollar, it can also push real estate values upward. With real estate investments you can keep ahead of the inflation, or at worst keep even.

At this point many of you are saying "No way, this guy is crazy." "A pipe dream!" While I realize that this investment program, based upon continued inflation, depends upon your faith that inflation will always be with us, the facts do support this premise. Let me demonstrate this.

Write down on a piece of paper what your income was this year, 10 years ago, 20 years ago and 30 years ago. If you have not been in the work market that long, then use your father's income. In another column write down the price of a commodity (like milk) that you are familiar with. The results, of course, will show huge price and wage increases. Refer to the Labor Department's Wage Statistics chart on page 25. There is no reason to believe that these increases won't continue. With a 10 per cent inflation rate, money in a 5 per cent bank savings account will cost you 5 per cent per year. With your money invested in real estate and using the leverage principle discussed in Chapter III, you can actually experience gains of 30 percent . . . 50 per cent . . . and even 100 per cent per year on your original investment dollar. That's how this program will help keep you ahead of inflation.

Buy Three More

Before making your three new purchases you must sell or refinance the second property that you bought at the end of the second year of the investment program. According to our inflation timetable you should sell the home for something between $52,000 and $53,000. On this hypothetical property you also have a $1,800 second which must be paid off. Allowing for a sales price of $52,700 with $4,000 for possible sales expenses, $1,800 on the second and a first loan of $31,500, you will end up with $15,400. Taking away another $1,500 for capital gains taxes you will have $13,900 ready for your next purchases.

Add to the $13,900 another $2,800 that you have accumulated each month by saving $50 plus tax savings on your properties. You now have $16,700 to buy three more properties, giving you a new grand total of six single family rental homes. Your three new purchases will be at $52,700 each.

For six years now I have asked you to put aside a fixed amount of money each month. This is necessary if you are buying property on a shoestring. With six properties now you don't have to do this any more unless you want to accumulate wealth at a far greater and faster rate than I am outlining here.

After six years you can begin to sit back and enjoy some of the fruits of property ownership. With three properties purchased two years ago at $43,500 and three more now at $52,700, you have a grand total of $288,600 in real estate (cost value) for income tax purposes (less about 20 per cent for the value of the lots which cannot be depreciated for tax purposes). Using the 3 1/3 per cent guideline we discussed earlier, you now have approximately $7,619 to deduct from your income taxes. If you are still in the 25 per cent tax bracket this means that you will now have $1,904 more to spend; $1,904 that would have gone to Uncle Sam if you had never purchased any rental properties.

Your Partner—Uncle Sam

To make this program work, I have told you that you should believe in continued inflation. You must also have faith that the U.S. Government will continue to support the residential home market.

At this writing, FHA will allow maximum loans of $60,000. On GI loans the limit is determined by the individual lender. Remember that FHA and GI loans are insured by Uncle Sam but the actual money comes from private sources. In 1970 the maximum FHA loan was only $33,000. Also in 1970 a buyer needed a $2,450 down payment to purchase a $30,000 home. In 1974 the government changed the FHA down payment ratio to allow a buyer to pay $1,250 down on a $30,000 home. Today an FHA buyer need pay only $1,000 down to buy the same priced home.

The point I am making is that the U.S. Government, being responsive to inflation, will continue to change and increase its program limits. I am confident that 20 years from now, when today's moderate priced home of $30,000 is selling for $100,000 or more there will still be a government program allowing for easy down payment purchases. For the investor this means a steady flow of good assumptions at whatever price. Future interest rates could possibly vary between 6 per cent and even 14 per cent. But high interest rates, even though they make it tougher for everyone, are not going to keep you from having a successful investment portfolio.

Eight Years Growth

At the end of year eight you now have six rental properties with a gross value of $382,362. Let's take a closer look.

● Purchase Numbers 3, 4, & 5 (after 4 years)

    Original purchase price $43,500

    Present Value   63,687
    Less present loan   37,500

    Value for each property   26,187

● Purchase Numbers 6, 7, & 8 (after 2 years)

    Original purchase price $52,700

    Present value   63,767
    Less present loan   46,700

    Value for each property   17,067

Total paper equity for six homes = $129,762

Mathematically, you can now see what is happening. At the end of six years you had four properties with a value of $63,312. With just two more years of 10 per cent appreciation, you have now increased your ownership to six homes and your equities have more than doubled to $129,762. "How sweet it is."

Sell 2 — Buy 4

After eight years of saving, buying with a limited amount of money and selling on a "get every penny" budget, I am now recommending that you slow down.

Why slow down? You don't have to! If you are one of those superhuman individuals that thrives on work and success, then go ahead and purchase three new properties for every one you sell. It can certainly be done by just following all the guidelines that I have set forth.

But if you are like most people there will be a limit to the number of hours you will want to spend with your investment program. Depending upon your degree of efficiency, you will find that each individual property will take you an average of between one and two hours each month for management. So with six properties you are already devoting between six and 12 hours per month and this does not include extra time necessary when you are buying or selling. If you must work for a living, your time will be limited, so you might want to consider slowing down your investment pace.

After eight years you will find yourself in a solid position. You have six homes and a lot of equity. And you will be paying a lot less in taxes, if any, to Uncle Sam. By selling two properties you will have a minimum of $40,000 available to purchase four new homes. Note that I have allowed nearly 10 per cent of the value ($6,187) for each home to be lost in selling costs. Again I remind you that if you sell with a lease-option contract, or if because of good tenants your property does not need a lot of refurbishing . . . then you can save a lot of this money allowed as "selling expenses."

Go ahead now and buy four more properties. For our purposes each one will be at a price of $63,500 with $9,500 paid down to assume the current loan. Yes, you probably can find good assumptions, even in the $60,000 price range, for $6,000 or $7,000 cash. But from now on I am going to show you how easy things can be.

After 10 Years

After 10 years you now have eight rental homes with a total value of over $615,000. More importantly you have over $230,000 in paper equities . . . or if you are a realist . . . you have $168,000 after subtracting approximate selling costs of 10 per cent for each home. You also have a tax deduction of over $12,000. Not bad for just $3,000 invested out of pocket plus $50 a month for six years! That's the way you play the monopoly game. Let's take a look.

- Purchase No. 5 (after six years)

Original purchase price	$43,500
Present value	77,060
less present loan	37,000
Equity	40,060

- Purchases No. 6,7,8 (after four years)

Original purchase price	52,700
Present Value	77,157
Less present loan	46,200
Equity for each home	30,957

- Purchase No. 9,10,11 & 12 (after two years)
  Original purchase price $63,500

  Present Value   76,835
  Less present loan   52,500

  Equity for each home   24,335

Total paper equity for eight homes = $230,271

Where To Next?

Each individual has a different reason for needing money. You might want security in old age whereas the next investor may want a nest egg for a trip to Europe, or a college education for his children.

Because each person has different desires and needs, I leave year 11 and each subsequent year up to your imagination. Here is an idea to start you thinking.

If you do not sell or buy any more properties after year 10, but keep them one more year, you will increase your equities from $230,000 to nearly $294,000. Eleven years from now your salary will probably be twice what it is today, but will it in one year equal $64,000 that your properties will earn for you?

IX

Bits & Pieces

Up to this point I have covered the basics. I have demonstrated what an investment program can mean in dollars and cents. Now that you have a rudimentary knowledge of the basic tools you will need for your investment program, it is time for graduate school. This chapter contains more advanced information on several important topics.

More Than One Way To Buy

As you have seen in the last chapter, it is possible without good luck, specialized knowledge or a great deal of beginning capital to build a nest egg of nearly $300,000. "Sounds great," you say. But it really isn't great.

That's right! If you are an alert investor you should make at least $100,000 more, or $400,000 in 11 years. There are two ways you can do this. The first method requires more beginning capital. The second methods requires more skillful buying and selling than we have described thus far.

I have developed our hypothetical investment program around a plan of $3,000 of beginning capital and a small monthly savings. I have done this to show that it can be done and to encourage the small investors with limited funds to get their feet wet. But just imagine what can be done if you start out with $10,000 or even $30,000. You may already be an investor. If you have a rental now and it has more than $15,000 spendable equity . . . get it out. Reinvest your equity on two or three new properties. Not only will they greatly increase your tax position but they will put you on the road to a $400,000 nest egg.

Here's a point worth mentioning. If you have a rental home valued at $30,000 in today's market, and if you keep the property for another 11 years it could be worth about $85,000. Not only is $85,000 (less the mortgage) a long shot from $300,000 or $400,000, but your tax base will be extremely low—being based upon the original purchase price. As you can see, buying, selling and refinancing are necessary for success.

The second method of stretching $300,000 into $400,000 is something that everyone can easily do. The purchases previously referred to were at market value. Many of your best assumption buys will be at market value and some will even be a little higher. But even so you should be able to make several purchases at prices considerably lower than market value.

Here are some ways to buy property below its true value. One of the most common ways is to find a rundown, dirty home that is selling for a price below market value. (This technique departs from my advice of only buying clean and near-perfect homes. This method should only be used, therefore, if you are a handy person and have the time to fix up the property.) After locating the rundown property, make a careful inspection so that you can be sure that there are no structural problems that you cannot handle. Secondly, make a ridiculously low offer. I find that many properties in the rundown category are unrealistically priced at near market value, but when they finally sell the price is often $5,000 to $7,000 under listed price. It may take two or three offers to buy such a home but when you get one you can make several thousand dollars with hardly more than a paint brush.

Another way to find a "steal" is to follow notices of default and foreclosure sales. In many states a deed of trust is used instead of a mortgage to secure the lender's rights until the loan is paid in full. From the lender's viewpoint the deed of trust is preferred because upon notice of default the debtor has a limited right of reinstatement of the loan, but no right of redemption after foreclosure as the sale is absolute.

Without belaboring the differences between mortgages and deeds of trust, it is important for you to know that publication of defaults must, according to law, be published prior to foreclosure sale. This gives you an exellent opportunity to contact the property owner to see if he would be interested in selling his property before he loses everything to foreclosure. While you may not find many ideal assumptions this way, it is an opportunity to find excellent buys at several thousand dollars below true market value.

In the county I live in all notices of default are printed in a publication called the "News Register." It contains no actual news items or advertisements but only data taken from the public records, such as bankruptcies, divorces, probates, mechanic's liens, etc. Anyone can subscribe to this publication.

100 Per Cent Financing

Imagine what would happen if you could buy real property for no money at all—at least no money out of pocket. You would become awfully rich—awfully fast—unless excessive negative cash flows held you back.

While very few investors always buy property with no money, you can be sure that many investors have bought at least some of their property this way.

This creative financing comes in two basic types. I'll refer to the first type as "Mickey Mouse" financing and the second type as 100 per cent financing.

Mickey Mouse financing is an old term—it was going out of use back in 1965 when I first went into real estate. The reason is simple—it is an illegal and dishonest method. Its use has been almost totally eliminated by real estate commissioners and the lending institutions.

Basically Mickey Mouse financing means agreeing to buy a property at a specific price (let's say $40,000) but then raising the price to $45,000 with the seller secretly kicking back $5,000 to the buyer. A neat way to buy property, but to pull it off you must hide all the material facts and figures from the lender. And in this type of transaction the seller is usually duped by the buyer along the way.

I only bring up the subject because you hear a lot about this method in the advertisements of some other real estate books and seminars. It is a risky method and I advise you to stay clear of it.

The second method of creative financing, however, is effective and quite acceptable. It is considered to be 100 per cent financing. You buy a property with a down payment that does not come out of your own pocket. It's your money, but it is a paper transaction (a second mortgage secured either by your residence or another rental).

Here is a hypothetical case study: You submit your best offer to buy a property, an offer in which the seller agrees to pay most of your closing costs and also agrees to carry back a second mortgage for half of your required down payment. (Incidentally, the seller might only agree to pay your closing costs if the price is raised $1,000 to cover them. This is okay since it is not a secret agreement which is being hidden from the lender.)

Now you've got your basic agreement, but you now need the other half of your down payment which we'll say is $4,000. This money (or in this case paper) will come from a second mortgage or trust deed secured by your residence or another investment property. Technically it does not even have to be a second mortgage secured by real property; it could be a bank loan secured by stocks, bonds, or other items of value that you own.

I've used this type of financing quite often, and it really works! Most conventional lenders will usually accept this type of financing. They would not let you borrow the $4,000 on just your good name, but they will allow you to take this money from something (like another property) that you already own. If you are using this 100 per cent financing method when assuming a government insured loan, you will not have to worry about what the lender's policy might be, because they cannot stop you.

New Kinds of Mortgages

A new type of conventional loan, called the variable rate mortgage, could soon have a big impact on the national real estate scene.

In 1975 VRM's, which have a fluctuating interest rate designed to rise and fall with the money market, accounted for 58 per cent of the loans made by five major California savings & loan associations. Bank of America and Wells Fargo Bank have also entered this field. Federal chartered savings & loans are currently prohibited from making VRM loans.

The VRM loans provide for a review of interest rates twice a year, with the possibilities of a modest charge either up or down as indicated by the cost of money at the time of each review.

In every instance of an increase in interest (which cannot ever exceed 2½ per cent over the original rate), the borrower will have 90 days from the date of the notice to pay off the loan, or any part of the loan without a prepayment charge. Most important for investors is that the VRM is fully assumable upon sale with no change in the then-existing interest rate. However, the lender must approve the buyer's credit.

Other innovative mortgage ideas may be on the way, too. The Federal Home Loan Bank Board, which regulates 86 per cent of the nation's savings and loan associations, is working on a comprehensive study of new types of mortgages. Many of their ideas are expected to get the green light — and when they do you can look for increased real estate sales of all kinds.

These new mortgages would include the GRADUATED PAY-MENT plan which is aimed at young people who expect their income to rise. With this type of mortgage the monthly payments will begin low and then increase progressively over the next four to six years.

Another type, called the REVERSE ANNUITY mortgage, would enable older people to put the equity in their houses to work providing retirement income. In essence, the homeowner would take out a series of monthly loans using his house as collateral.

Closing Costs

It seems that closing costs (also known as settlement charges) are getting higher all the time. One reason, of course, is that the higher sales prices go, the higher closing costs go, too. It is not uncommon for a typical home buyer to pay as much as $2,000 in closing costs on a $35,000 purchase. These high tariffs could drive a potential investor right out of the market. I say could . . . not will . . . because I don't expect you to ever have to pay more than a few hundred dollars.

Buyers closing costs include many things, with the "big three" cost items being title insurance, loan fee, and tax and insurance impounds. When you assume an FHA or GI loan the only one of these charges that you will have is title insurance. And in many areas this cost is split with the seller. There is no loan fee on an assumption—only a relatively small loan assumption fee.

As for the tax and insurance impounds, this charge can almost always be successfully avoided. As part of your deposit receipt or contract to purchase, insist in writing that "buyers to assume sellers tax and insurance impound account and all payments are to be current." This means that the seller will leave whatever impound balance he has for you. It may only be $200 but if you do not ask for and get the impounds your costs could include six months of taxes and one year prepaid insurance.

When you assume the tax and insurance trust funds you obviously inherit whatever insurance policy the seller had on the property. After the sale is completed you may want to increase the amount of fire coverage, eliminate costly homeowner benefits or even cancel the policy and write a new one with your own insurance agent. Don't forget to increase your amount of insurance every few years as the value of the property increases.

While closing costs are relatively low on an assumption, you can expect to pay quite a lot when obtaining a new conventional loan. The difference is that you will have a loan fee from 1 to 2½ per cent of the loan amount plus the tax and insurance impounds in many cases. Most of these charges can be legally avoided, however, by having the seller pay these. Check with your lender. Most will allow the seller to pay the loan fee but not the impounds. Negotiate with the seller. In your offer to purchase write "Seller to pay buyer's loan fee, not to exceed 1½ points" or write "seller to pay all buyer's non-recurring closing costs not to exceed $1,000."

In the second example, I limited the amount to $1,000 because I find that most sellers want all costs in black and white. They don't want loose ends that could mean paying $500 or $1,000 or even $1,500. Non-recurring closing costs, incidentally, refer to all the costs that are only applicable when you buy the property. Recurring costs are your tax and insurance costs which are charged each year.

Closing costs for a seller are considerably less than those of the buyer, except when a costly prepayment penalty is included. FHA and GI loans, however, have no prepayment clauses. So in most cases, the seller will be facing only a few hundred dollars in selling costs.

Where Not To Buy Property

In Chapter IV, I discussed the principles of "Location, Condition, and Financing." I stressed buying a clean, well-kept home in a good neighborhood. At this point, I think it is prudent to discuss "location" in even greater depth.

A carefully planned investment program can succeed in any area of the United States, whether it be in city, country or suburban properties. But the general location of your properties is important. I am not referring to individual subdivisions but to larger geographical areas.

While you can be successful with single family investments in a large city, your best bet is a fast growing suburban community. Your chances are obviously better in a steadily growing community with accompanying pressure for new and used homes. And don't overlook small-town America, as most of these communities can be great locations for your investment portfolio.

On the flip side of the coin, however, are America's large inner cities . . . some of which are decaying and some rebuilding. Money can be made with inner city real estate, but only by the experts who are well schooled in redevelopment procedures or in "slum landlord" techniques. The principles outlined in this book were not developed for inner city property or problems.

In addition to inner city property, be very cautious of what can be considered fringe neighborhoods. These can be areas that are close to big cities but not quite suburban. Most of the residents could be considered upper lower class. About half of the residents own their own home while the other half rent. There are several problems you would need to face as a landlord in a fringe location, one of the main ones being crime. I know of a community like this, only 20 miles from my office; as soon as a home is vacated all the windows get broken the first night it is empty.

The second problem would be chronic unemployment. The residents of these poor communities are going to be among the first — and hardest — hit whenever unemployment shifts upwards.

As you can see — location is important. But no matter where you live you will be near good places to invest your money.

Cluster Homes

Many real estate experts believe that America's living habits are changing. With smaller families, higher building costs, etc., many new types of housing units have sprung up throughout the United States. These new developments can be duplexes, duets, townhouses, garden homes or condominiums.

The important difference is that they are not one living unit on one clearly defined lot. They are space savers designed basically for the small family.

In the first two editions of *The Monopoly Game* I warned the investor to be very wary when considering the so-called cluster home. It turns out that I was both right . . . and wrong. For example: In the Miami-Fort Lauderdale metropolitan housing market nearly 28,000 new condos remained unsold during the first part of 1976. But in the Los Angeles-Orange County market condos were selling so fast that some developers had to use a lottery system. At the same time Philadelphia's condo market was stagnant but Detroit's was moving at a good pace.

Why the discrepancies? I'll take a stab at the answer. From first-hand experience I have found out that most buyers and renters want a private yard and covered garage. Only the most expensive cluster homes adequately provide these. This theory is upheld by a national survey of potential home buying families in 1976, according to *Banker* magazine. The survey showed that 93 out of 100 would seek a detached single-family house. According to the survey, "The American dream remains intact: A single-family home with enough property to guarantee some privacy. Despite some predictions to the contrary by demographers and others, Bureau of Census statistics show, according to the Research Department of the National Association of Realtors, the demand for detached single-family homes remains strong and possibly is growing stronger."

So, when given a choice between equally attractive accommodations, most buyers and renters will choose the single-family home. But in a fast moving real estate market in which home prices are rapidly escalating, many people will choose the cluster homes out of necessity. This is what has happened in California. The condo market dramatically turned around because single-family homes were appreciating between 15 and 25 per cent each year beginning in early 1975.

Another factor is overbuilding. When sales are brisk and interest rates are low, the developers lay plans for the next year. The result is often too many new units are built and the market must be given time to assimilate them. Until the units are assimilated, sales will be slow.

If you are considering buying cluster homes, be sure and double-check their track record in your community. Make sure that they are appreciating in value as much as a comparable single family home.

Duplexes

Many investors have asked me about duplexes. Duplexes do not really fall into the category of single family home or multi-family investments.

Some consider duplexes the first step on the way to four units and then eight units and so on. For the purposes of this book, however, I suggest you consider a duplex as a single family home. But before buying one—give it the following tests.

First of all, is the property in a neighborhood which will attract a future buyer who would be an owner-occupant? If the neighborhood is on the downswing or is in a so-called "zoning buffer" between commercial property and apartments—then forget it.

Secondly, is the duplex capable of selling as fast as a home in a comparable and nearby residential neighborhood? Ask your Realtor to check on it. He should have comparable sales figures which will show if the duplex market is dragging or not. If all signs are go, then treat the duplex exactly as you would a single family home.

Investment Groups

Many people have banded together in groups for investment purposes. Two people can form a partnership. For larger groups a limited partnership might be the best answer.

Several years ago I helped form an investment group. After five years we had 10 members and four rental homes. The group was a lot of fun but not really profitable. We finally ended the partnership and liquidated our properties.

I do not recommend investment groups for single family home investing. You can do the job better yourself. If you have limited capital you can start small and then use the principle of leverage to expand your holdings. "Too many cooks spoil the broth," is a very true statement when applied to investment groups. In groups people tend to sit back and expect the other guy to do the work.

If you do form a group, however, put everything in writing and consult an attorney and tax accountant so that you get off on the right foot.

Syndicates

Many of the problems inherent in an investment group can be eliminated by forming a syndicate. Most syndicates are limited partnerships in which the general partner(s) completely runs the group's business. The limited partners contribute the capital to the syndicate but have no real voice in conducting business.

In this manner those with the knowledge and interest in running the partnership can do so while those members who are only interested in a return on their investment dollar may be free of problems.

The major disadvantage of syndicates is the legal red tape, both federal and state, that one will encounter.

But they can nevertheless be a real springboard for an ambitious investor. He can set himself up as the sole general partner and then enlist up to 10 friends or relatives to be the limited partners whose only involvement would be a one-time cash contribution.

The general partner does not need to contribute any cash to the syndicate. While it is operating he may receive management fees for his time and expenses and when the syndicate closes out he can receive up to 25 per cent of the equities and/or profit. In most states the general partner does not need a real estate license to do all of this. It's a nice way to create profit for everyone—the general partner as well as the limited partners who might not have ever gotten involved with rental property had it not been for the syndicate.

It can be sweet but it is also highly sophisticated; too much so for me to go into the complete details here. However, Impact Publishing Company is marketing monthly in-depth reports which will cover in greater detail this and many other exciting investment ideas. Details are explained in the back of this book.

Property Management

If you are a would-be investor in the "sounds great but I don't have the time" category, you should seriously consider professional property management. I don't recommend management to all investors. And I say this as the former owner of a property management company.

There is a time and place for everything! If you have the time, the interest and an objective outlook then you should personally look after your own properties. Property management cannot replace the personal touch of a careful and wise investor. If you don't have the time, you should consider a qualified property manager. Usually the fees are not too high and they are tax deductible.

If you are the type of individual who becomes emotionally involved with your properties and tenants, you should seriously consider property management. You must be objective about your investments.

As an investor you should look at your property from two standpoints: 1. What is the real yield going to be if your portfolio is managed by someone else? 2. What will the yield be if you do your own management, realizing with more than two or three homes you in effect will have a part-time job? Often the difference in yield isn't that great and thus property management may be the answer.

Many corporation executives that should get into a rental program don't because they do not have the time or they are worried about being transferred. If you are in this situation, don't let it stop you. Use property management services and invest.

Reducing Capital Gains Tax

The subject of taxes, especially capital gains treatment, is very complex. Very few people have the same tax situation. In Chapter VIII, I allowed $1,500 in taxes to be paid after each sale. This figure is somewhat arbitrary and over-simplified. Some investors will be in a position to pay no tax where another investor might be saddled with a $3,000 tax. With capital gains the more you earn the more you pay, but never do you pay more than 50 per cent of the gain.

For example, if you sell a property for $50,000 you must determine your gain by first subtracting your acquisition cost (ex: $30,000); major improvements and repairs through the years (ex: $1,000) and your selling costs (ex: $4,000). This leaves you with a gain of $15,000. Divide this figure in half. You now have $7,500 subject to tax. Whether you pay nothing, or $1,000 or $3,000 depends upon your total taxable income position for the particular tax year.

With careful planning you can greatly lessen your tax burden. For instance, if you are selling a property in order to buy three new ones, do so in January or February. In this way, you will be able to depreciate three new properties for most of a year. This technique will allow you to reduce your $7,500 profit by as much as $2,000 to $4,000, depending, of course, upon the new sales prices.

I have recommended that you sell or refinance each property after four years of ownership. In order to reduce your tax bite when selling you may find it necessary to vary the four-year rule. If you are having an excellent income year you may need to wait an additional year so the taxes won't take away too much profit. Conversely, if you are having a particularly poor income year, you may want to sell early to protect your profit. Be sure to have a good tax adviser — it may save you a lot of money in the long run.

You must expect to pay some capital gains tax in the early stages of your investment program. But later on — after you have accumulated eight or more properties — you should have enough tax shield so that you can sell one property a year without paying any taxes. This works well unless your income is too high or until you reduce your inventory so low that you lose your shield. You can replenish your shield, however, by taking a small part of the proceeds from a sale and reinvesting in a high loan balance assumption.

Exchanging

I am not going to go into the techniques of so-called tax free exchanges because it is a method seldom used in residential property investing. But it is important for you to know that it is a method you might some day use to maximize and retain equity and at the same time defer capital gain taxes.

After you have accumulated eight or more residential properties you may want to move into multi-unit investments. You can do this by trading up for multi-units. Not only will a trade give you a strong new tax basis but you will retain most of your equity as you will not have an immediate tax, loan discount points or most of the other selling expenses that were discussed earlier.

The Golden Years

The following is a true story and one too often repeated.

A mother of 10 children was widowed after 40 years of marriage. During that time her husband had been earning between $45,000 and $60,000 annually and had an international reputation in his field. All of the children worked their way through college.

But what did the husband leave his wife? Less than $2,000 in bonds, $20,000 in life insurance and house payments that had 20 years to go. With inflation, house payments and all she is having a difficult time.

The children are wonderful and they all try to help. But she deeply resents the fact that after 40 years of devotion, she NEEDS help.

Statistics tell us that most wives outlive their husbands. Something must be done to help these widows. Life insurance isn't the answer. It will help, all right; it might even pay the bills for a year or two. The stock market is capable of terrific slumps. Social security, contrary to popular belief, is not the answer either.

Our social security system is headed for trouble (*Time*, February 16, 1976) and what payments are received really just amount to peanuts.

"Some people think that if they've always earned the maximum amount covered by social security they will get the highest benefit shown on the chart," according to a publication printed by the U.S. Department of Health, Education and Welfare. "That isn't so. The most a person reaching 65 in 1975 can get is $341.70. The reason is that the maximum amount of earnings covered by social security was lower in past years than it is now. Those years of lower limits must be counted in with the higher ones of recent years to figure your average earnings and thus the amount of your monthly retirement check." If you are used to $1,000 a month or more income, good luck on adjusting to $341.70.

And the story of survivor benefits is even bleaker! For a dependent wife at age 62, the maximum payment is $192.10. And don't get excited if she was also a worker because according to HEW, "if a woman is eligible for both a worker's benefit and a wife's benefit, the check actually payable is limited to the larger of the two."

Company or union retirement programs can be a helpful supplement to social security. But there is an even better idea. It's a 20-year program (Follow Chapter VIII, "Pyramiding Your Equities" for the first 11 years) which involves a combination of rental homes and second deeds of trust (mortgages). After 20 years you can easily have eight rental homes plus more than $250,000 in seconds which will earn you more than $25,000 a year.

There is too much to be said about seconds for just one section of one chapter. It's a complete story in itself. To tell this story I have completed a book which is now on the market. It's called:

HOW TO GROW A MONEYTREE
The Magical Book of Making Big Money
With Second Mortgages

As I pointed out earlier, there is not a better investment around than single family homes for making a great deal of money in a relatively short time period. But if you are looking at retirement 20 years down the road, you might not want to be saddled with 30 or so rental homes just about the time of life you want to travel.

"Moneytree" will show you an alternate route — a way to retire in relative ease with just a few homes for tax shelter but a lot of cash coming in each month from your seconds. The book will explain how and when to buy seconds at discounts of 25 per cent and more; how to originate new seconds; what legal clauses you must be aware of; how to make easy collections; plus many other important facts that will enable you to pyramid your initial investments into a small fortune. "Moneytree" sells for $9.95. You will find a handy order blank at the back of this book.

X

A Word About Realtors

If you are actively engaged in the real estate profession, then this chapter is written for you. But if you are not a licensee—don't go away, because the first part tells how to go about finding your super agent; the professional man or woman who will make you money without wasting your valuable time.

Finding Your Agent

One of my favorite subjects is real estate salesmen. In over eight years as the owner of a realty firm employing an average of 10 salespeople, I have personally witnessed the actions of both excellent and horrible agents. Some were earning $40,000 per year and more while others were canned after going six months without a sale.

What makes the difference? There is no easy answer but from my many years of observation I came to the following conclusions. Most good agents have several things in common, among which are a willingness to put in more than 40 hours of work each week, and to change bad habits and develop new and better habits. The good agents are also motivated to make a lot of money . . . but they understand that to do this they must provide quality service to their clients, which in turn results in repeat business and new referral clients.

If you will excuse the stereotyping, most bad (or unproductive) salespeople have the following qualities in common: They are lazy and do not make any serious attempts to change their ways or learn prescribed sales techniques. They may have a desire to make good money but they don't have the strong motivation of the better agent. While they understand that quality client service brings repeat business they just don't take the time. To such people, being paid a commission is more important than doing a complete and professional job.

You can almost always recognize poor sales people by their sloppy attitude . . . or instant sales pressure whenever their client gives them the slightest of buying signals. If you are not really sure which category an agent falls into, just ask him how many sales and listings he has procured in the past 3 months. If the answer is two or less—watch out.

Give the new salespeople a break, however. It may take them six months or so to get rolling. But once they do they might be quite good. You will probably find that a new agent is willing to work much harder for you than one that has been around for several years.

As I mentioned before, your best bet is to find one salesperson that you trust and enjoy working with. Once you find that person— stick with him or her.

But if you haven't found that perfect agent yet (one that is honest, hardworking and knowledgeable) then here are a few ideas that might help. First of all find a friend or business acquaintance that is very happy with their agent. Ask for an introduction. Many of the best agents get better than 75 per cent of their business from referrals.

If that idea does not work then telephone the broker of an office which you suspect will be good. Tell the broker that you have read *The Monopoly Game* and you are looking for an experienced and investment-oriented agent to help you. Insist on a good agent—not necessarily the one currently on floor duty. Keep in mind that out of every 10 agents working for a typical company, probably only three or four will really be good. It's a sad but true fact. In most communities over 75 per cent of new agents fall by the wayside in their first year.

You will find that you will have better results with a REALTOR than with a licensed but non-Realtor agent. Realtors and Realtor Associates are members of both local boards and the National Association of Realtors. Thus they are the only ones that have access to multiple listing services.

Retirement

If you are a career real estate salesperson, ask yourself this question: "How many more years before I retire and when I do retire how am I going to live?" If you worked for a bank, the government, a large company or corporation, the question would be answered. You would then have a definite age to retire and a definite retirement program which would pay you x amount of dollars for the rest of your life.

As a real estate agent you must protect yourself. Nobody is going to do it for you. One advantage of our industry is that you can work as much or as little as you want. If you are physically able at age 70, you can continue to work and provide an income. But how about your state of affairs if you are unable to continue working or if you just plain don't want to work any longer?

The answer is obvious. If you intend to make real estate your career, you must invest for future retirement. If you work in the commercial end of real estate, then you should invest in that field which you know best. If you are in the largest group of salesmen, however, and work in residential sales, you should invest in rental homes. Always do what you know best.

Your residential investments can cover three basic areas: 1. Single family homes as described herein; 2. Second mortgages; and 3. Speculation purchases and resale of same.

Retirement is not your only reason for an investment program. As you know, real estate sales can greatly fluctuate because of changes in mortgage rates and availability of money. Many a real estate salesperson survived the slumps of 1966 and 1974 by selling a rental property. Another nice advantage is the more properties you own the more income you can keep. Largely due to my investment portfolio, I can earn up to $30,000 now without paying any taxes (state and federal) except for the social security self-employment tax.

Built-In Advantages

As a salesperson working day in and day out in real estate, you have many advantages over most investors. These advantages will help you make more money. And these advantages make for even more reasons why you cannot afford to be without an investment portfolio of rental properties. Some of these advantages are:

1. *Knowledge of market values:* As a working Realtor you will know the values of almost every property you come in contact with. And if you don't know the value you can easily find out by going to your office or Board of Realtor comparative value files. This knowledge will give you a great advantage as you won't need to waste time in researching values.

2. *Knowledge of market conditions:* Another Realtor advantage is the fact that you are constantly on top of any interest or loan discount changes. An experienced Realtor will also be able to spot trends that will help him make money.

3. *Exposure to Listings:* A very important advantage for the Realtor is that he is exposed to hundreds of listings. Often this will be a personal lead on a property coming up for sale. This means, of course, that the real estate salesman can have first crack at a good buy. But be careful, as there are pitfalls I will explain later in this chapter.

4. *Easier Maintenance:* A Realtor should have a long list of qualified and inexpensive handymen, gardeners, painters, plumbers, etc. It is probable, too, that a salesman's rental properties will be near his place of employment. This means that when a problem arises he can easily drop by the home to take care of it. Most non-Realtor investors have a job they can't leave, or work several miles away. This means that the problem may have to wait until evening or a weekend.

5. *Commissions:* Naturally, receiving compensation when selling or buying is a big Realtor advantage over the regular investor.

6. *Selling the tenant:* Here is an advantage to strive for. To date, I have sold five of my previous tenants a new home. Thus by owning rental property I have been able to make an additional bonus. As a Realtor you have an extra incentive to be a good landlord. When I lease a property I am always looking for a potential home buyer. Before they even move into my property I offer them an opportunity to break their lease if they buy a home through me. Of course, this approach is not recommended to the non-Realtor investor.

Selling The Investor

Many Realtors derive a fairly high percentage of their income from sales to investors. To be successful with investors a salesperson should have a full understanding of market values, investment principles and rental management and maintenance problems. This information is a start, but that's not all that you'll need.

You must also be a person of high ethical values. Many people, because of a bad experience, do not trust real estate agents. They expect the worst. The investor expects his Realtor, as well as all the others in the area, to beat him to the punch every time a good new listing pops up. This sad fact discourages many would-be investors. What I am going to do is to advise you to give up one of your advantages.

Tell each of the investors you work with that you will give him first crack at any new listing. Tell him that you personally won't buy the property until he has had a chance himself. This doesn't mean you must wait forever. When you discover a good listing, call your investor, but don't give him more than 24 hours.

A workable technique that I have used to control a property that I want is to write on the deposit receipt after *buyer* the following: "David Glubetich or his asignee." I put up the earnest money deposit and fully expect to buy the property but leave an opening to assign the contract (with all identical terms) to one of my investors. In this way you don't have to worry about losing a good buy while you call on your list of investors. If none of my investors want the property, I get a good buy. If an investor does take over, I make a commission.

A warm, friendly and honest relationship will pay off—and not just with investors.

If you don't have any investors, or have just a few—develop some. I recommend keeping a list of all potential investors. Among other things your list must contain both work and home phone numbers, type of property wanted, income and amount of cash available, and a note as to whether or not the investor is capable of fixing up "dirty dogs." You'll increase the names on the list every few weeks from contacts you make or ad calls you receive. Then when a good investment buy comes along, call everyone on your list, starting first with your most valued clients. If a would-be investor shows no interest after four or five calls, then strike his name off your list.

If your investor is looking for small cash-outlay assumptions, remind him to check the local newspaper for "For Sale by Owner" ads. This may sound like strange advice from one Realtor to another. But here are the facts: First of all, he is probably doing so anyway. He will appreciate your honesty. Secondly, when it comes to $2,000 and $3,000 FHA and GI assumptions, the "For Sale by Owner" *is* a prime source. Thirdly, a continued relationship with many future listing and sales commissions is more important than just one now. If you are truly going to be of service to your investor, you must be thoroughly honest and not come off as "another greedy real estate salesman."

Your Office

Each real estate office has an office policy which is probably unlike any other. The terms of your Broker-Salesman Contract and policy manual can be quite important if you intend to invest in real property.

If you are Broker-Owner there really is no problem as you will be the one who determines policy. But if you are not the owner, your investment desires can be aided or hurt by office procedures. I know of one broker who does not allow his salesmen to make any real estate investments. There is no salesman-investor conflict this way but the salespeople greatly suffer because they cannot enter into the great home investment bonanza.

The point I am making is simple. If you intend to invest in property, then select an office that has a liberal policy regarding investment purchases by salespeople.

Conclusion

I know of one family which owns more than 50 rental homes. They started when their children were very young—and now the children are in college. For this family their investment portfolio means much more than just income and retirement. It is a family activity. Many hundreds of hours were invested by all in scrubbing, painting and readying property for the next tenant. For them their rentals became a wonderful way of life.

Your rental properties can make you a lot of money and give you a lot of security. And just maybe they can help to change your life, too. Embarking on a new venture can bring you new outlooks, new friends and perhaps a new hobby.

Thousands of people are now investing in single family homes. I don't believe that any one of them would do so if they did not enjoy it or receive some type of personal satisfaction. Buying and selling homes is largely a do-it-yourself investment program. The more pride you take in your work the more successful you will be.

If you like the ideas I have presented—then get your feet wet—NOW. Don't put it off. You're now better equipped with knowledge than I was when I bought my first property.

You'll enjoy it and profit in many, many ways.

How Would You Like To Double . . .
Or Even Triple Your Investment Profit?

Double or triple profit!! Absurd as this may sound to you now there is a way it can be done. Sure, not everybody has a strong enough motivation to become RICH . . . not everyone has the time to make more money than they are making now. BUT FOR THOSE WHO ARE WILLING TO LISTEN . . . TO LEARN . . . AND TO TRY . . . THERE ARE ALWAYS MORE WAYS TO DRAMATI-CALLY INCREASE PROFITS.

The Secrets of Success

Why is it that some people make a killing in real estate, some just plug along making a decent profit while still others get discouraged and quit after just a year or two?? The answer is really simple. It's primarily a mental problem—success or failure is controlled by your own attitudes. You will see what I mean when you read the following FIVE SECRETS OF SUCCESS.

1. BELIEVE IT WILL HAPPEN: Inflation has always been with us and always will be with us. You must sincerely believe this. You must believe that today's $50,000 home will be worth $150,000 in the future—if not in 10 years then in 20 years.

2. BUY! BUY! BUY!: You must buy as many properties as you can with the smallest down payments possible if you really want to make big money. True, we all have financial and physical limitations—but those who can find ways to overcome those limitations in order to buy the most properties will make the most money in the shortest time.

3. DON'T GET DISCOURAGED: Property ownership brings problems, but the great majority of them will be small. The successful investor will not let himself be discouraged with nagging problems, but will instead learn from them and resolve to never let them happen again. If you can learn from your mistakes you will then be on the road to success.

4. KEEP YOUR EQUITIES IN REAL ESTATE: Set a financial goal and then stick to it. Keep your equities in real estate; whether you sell or refinance a property keep your money going with bigger and better purchases. You must pyramid to really get

rich. Taking money out of your portfolios for European vacations, etc. can be lots of fun but you won't become successful as quickly.

5. LEARN EVERYTHING YOU CAN: Learn from your own experiences. But don't stop there—set aside just one hour each week and read everything about real estate that you can get your hands on. When you meet someone who is successfully investing in real estate (or any other field for that matter) pick his brains. Find out what other successful people are doing, because just one new idea could bring you a $10,000 profit someday.

Introducing A New Service
That Will Show You—Step By Step
How To Make Bigger Profits Than You Ever
Dreamed Possible

In both *THE MONOPOLY GAME* and *HOW TO GROW A MONEYTREE* I strived to give you the motivation . . . and basic knowledge . . . you will need to successfully embark upon your own investment program. The principles in the books work . . . for almost anyone . . . and in nearly every community. But I am just one person! IMAGINE HOW SUCCESSFUL YOU COULD BE IF THERE WAS A WAY TO TAP THE BRAINS OF THE BEST AND MOST KNOWLEDGEABLE MEN AND WOMEN IN THE REAL ESTATE AND FINANCIAL FIELDS. It could be comparable to tapping the mind of the late J. Paul Getty along with others of equal stature. What you would gain could not be accurately translated into dollar value—but it would be nearly priceless.

Impact Publishing Company, the people responsible for my two books, has been searching the U.S. for the best real estate brains available. Many are already hard at work putting their knowledge and special expertise down on paper. Their works will be made available in a series of monthly in-depth reports. These Impact Reports are a series of hard-hitting minibooks which will show you step by step how to make a lot of money in real estate.

These Impact Reports are truly impressive. THEY ARE UNLIKE ANYTHING ELSE YOU'VE EVER READ OR HEARD ABOUT! Each one is over 6,000 words . . . and many are over 10,000. Each one is devoted to a single subject. No superficial scratching of the surface . . . only complete, practical ideas that you can use to improve (and add to) your investment portfolios. And each one is written by an expert in his or her field . . . not professional writers but the best WORKING real estate brains from Oregon to Florida.

124

Each author is selected for his ability to clearly provide worthwhile information that will show the reader how to make and save money with their real estate investments. All topics covered by Impact Reports will be geared toward the small and mid-sized investors that are into single family and small multiple units. THERE WILL BE NO REPORTS ISSUED ON OVERLY COMPLICATED TOPICS LIKE INDUSTRIAL PARKS OR SHOPPING CENTERS.

Here are just a few of the exciting subjects coming your way:

- How to steal a house
  (the first scheduled report by
  Phoenix Realtor Dan Schwartz)
- How to profit with contracts of sale
- What you need to know about evictions
- How to buy property in tight money markets
- How to successfully invest in small multiple income properties
- How to buy rundown properties and turn a quick profit
- Proven methods of dealing with obnoxious tenants
- How to buy property with nothing down
- New tax saving ideas
- How to make big money with syndicates

When you subscribe to this new service . . . you will get a lot more than just the Impact Reports. As a bonus you will receive an UPDATE with each report. The UPDATE is a small newsletter that will keep you informed on what's happening in the real estate investment world. It will give you a valuable overview of the whole investment market . . . and it will steer you clear of trouble spots and guide you to where the money is being made.

And that's still not all! As a subscriber to Impact Reports you will be offered special discounts on a wide selection of real estate books . . . many up to 50 per cent off list price. Not only books from Impact Publishing Company (like *The Monopoly Game*) but best selling books from many large national publishers.

Best of all . . . this new service is not expensive. For only $59 (tax deductible) you will receive a one-year subscription for 10 monthly reports plus 10 Updates plus numerous offers for excellent books at special discount prices. (Note: The July-August and November-December reports will be combined). If you are a bargain hunter you may subscribe for two years at only $99.

As you can see this new service (which gets under way in April, 1978) is not expensive. But if you are the ultra cautious type who thinks that anything over $2 costs too much . . . consider these facts: IF YOU ARE CURRENTLY INVESTING YOUR MONEY IN REAL ESTATE, I UNEQUIVOCALLY PROMISE YOU THAT YOU WILL BE BOMBARDED WITH HUNDREDS OF SUBSTANTIAL IDEAS FROM THESE REPORTS AND UPDATES. ANY ONE OF THESE NEW (OR NEGLECTED) IDEAS CAN HELP YOU MAKE . . . OR SAVE . . . ANYWHERE FROM $10 TO SEVERAL THOUSANDS OF DOLLARS.

What you must now do is make a decision. Remember—all great fortunes began with a simple decision to take action! An old Chinese proverb states: "A journey of a thousand miles begins with the first step." If you have any reservations about Impact Reports, I am going to make it easier for you to make your decision. IF YOU ARE NOT COMPLETELY SATISFIED AFTER YOU RECEIVE YOUR FIRST TWO REPORTS AND UPDATES, IMPACT PUBLISHING COMPANY WILL REFUND YOUR MONEY—IN FULL. THAT'S RIGHT . . . BETWEEN THE SECOND AND THIRD MONTH YOU MAY CANCEL AND RECEIVE A FULL REFUND AND FOR YOUR TROUBLE YOU MAY KEEP WHAT YOU WERE ALREADY SENT.

You have nothing to lose but perhaps a great deal to gain. See the following order form so you can get started now. Incidentally, as a subscriber you will be offered previous Impact Reports that you may have missed for only $2 each, as long as the supply lasts.

IMPACT REPORT
ORDER FORM

Yes, I would like to tap the brains of some of the best real estate investors in the country. Please enter my subscription to Real Estate Investing IMPACT REPORTS. I understand that I will also receive an UPDATE newsletter with each report.

NAME
_____

ADDRESS
_____

CITY
_____

STATE AND ZIP
_____

FOR CREDIT CARD
ORDERS SIGN HERE
_____

☐ Master Charge ☐ Visa ☐ Bankamericard

CREDIT CARD
NUMBER _____

EXPIRATION
DATE _____

☐ One year subscription for $59 ☐ Two years subscription for $99

Amount Enclosed $ _____

MAIL TO:
IMPACT PUBLISHING COMPANY
12 Gregory Lane
Pleasant Hill, California 94523

IMPACT REPORT
ORDER FORM

Yes, I would like to tap the brains of some of the best real estate investors in the country. Please enter my subscription to Real Estate Investing IMPACT REPORTS. I understand that I will also receive an UPDATE newsletter with each report.

NAME _____

ADDRESS _____

CITY _____

STATE AND ZIP _____

FOR CREDIT CARD
ORDERS SIGN HERE _____

☐ Master Charge   ☐ Visa   ☐ Bankamericard

CREDIT CARD
NUMBER _____

EXPIRATION
DATE _____

☐ One year subscription   ☐ Two years subscription
    for $59   for $99

Amount Enclosed $ _____

MAIL TO:
IMPACT PUBLISHING COMPANY
12 Gregory Lane
Pleasant Hill, California 94523

IMPACT REPORT
ORDER FORM

Yes, I would like to tap the brains of some of the best real estate investors in the country. Please enter my subscription to Real Estate Investing IMPACT REPORTS. I understand that I will also receive an UPDATE newsletter with each report.

NAME _____

ADDRESS _____

CITY _____

STATE AND ZIP _____

FOR CREDIT CARD
ORDERS SIGN HERE _____

☐ Master Charge   ☐ Visa   ☐ Bankamericard

CREDIT CARD
NUMBER _____

EXPIRATION
DATE _____

☐ One year subscription   ☐ Two years subscription
   for $59   for $99

Amount Enclosed $ _____

MAIL TO:
IMPACT PUBLISHING COMPANY
12 Gregory Lane
Pleasant Hill, California 94523

MONOPOLY GAME and MONEYTREE
ORDER FORM

Please send _____ copies of *The Monopoly Game* by D. Glubetich

_____ copies of *How to Grow A Moneytree*

NAME _____

ADDRESS _____

CITY _____

STATE AND ZIP _____

FOR CREDIT CARD
ORDERS SIGN HERE _____

☐ Master Charge   ☐ Visa   ☐ BankAmericard

Credit Card Number _____

Expiration Date _____

Price: $9.95 per single copy.

Amount Enclosed $_____

Combination orders are accepted
with the following discounts:

3 to 4 books @ $7.50 each
5 to 9 books @ $6.50 each
10 to 19 books @ $6.00 each

(Please call for further discounts)

MAIL TO:
IMPACT PUBLISHING COMPANY
12 Gregory Lane
Pleasant Hill, California 94523

Telephone (415) 689-5090

MONOPOLY GAME and MONEYTREE
ORDER FORM

Please send _____copies of *The Monopoly Game* by D. Glubetich

_____copies of *How to Grow A Moneytree*

NAME _____

ADDRESS _____

CITY _____

STATE AND ZIP _____

FOR CREDIT CARD
ORDERS SIGN HERE _____

☐ Master Charge   ☐ Visa   ☐ BankAmericard

Credit Card Number _____

Expiration Date _____

Price: $9.95 per single copy.

Amount Enclosed $_____

Combination orders are accepted
with the following discounts:

3 to 4 books @ $7.50 each
5 to 9 books @ $6.50 each
10 to 19 books @ $6.00 each

(Please call for further discounts)

MAIL TO:
IMPACT PUBLISHING COMPANY
12 Gregory Lane
Pleasant Hill, California 94523

Telephone (415) 689-5090

About The Author

David Glubetich, 39, was born in Oakland, California. A graduate of San Jose State College with a degree in journalism/public relations, he turned to real estate in 1965 after four years of Chamber of Commerce work. After two years he obtained his broker's license and two years later in 1969 he purchased Wells Realty in Pleasant Hill, California.

In addition to Wells Realty, a firm which specializes in residential sales, he formerly owned Home Management Services, a company designed to manage single family homes for investors.

He is now dividing his time between real estate sales and writing. He is planning to write a third real estate book in the near future.